Blaine

The inside workings
of my mind — at least
the better side.

Dwayne

THE WAY IN

SAGA SONGS AND STAR OF JESUS

W.C. FIPKE

ISBN 978-0-9951925-0-8
Publication titled THE WAY IN - saga songs and star of jesus
COPYRIGHT by W.C. Fipke dated June 1, 2016 IN KELOWNA, B.C., CANADA

I

silence
the way in
dark silence
echoes in the darkness
behind the boulder door blackness
an empty hole in the echo
crawl into the cave
inside the quiet chamber
inside the rock tomb
the silent room the silent womb
no body in the darkness
a smell of stillness stays silent
breathless still silent still
touch around solid rock
below a loose rock and dirt floor
bones and a body buried under
dig up the dust dirt dreams
awaken the ground memories
smell imagination
treasure imagination coming out of darkness
a treasure of buried imagination appears
a scroll of gold stories found
sight opens words unroll
a scroll unrolls
a body comes to life in the words
a song comes to life
each word a note
echoes between each word
silence between each word
images come to life
sounds of life come out
through the words
found in the womb
the savior of silence sings
*

my heartbeats
count seven times
a rhythm of seven beats
one direction glowing deep
then seven beats another direction
eager
an echo of a distant heartbeat
the echo not from my heart
the far heartbeat leads the rhythm
four heartbeats in a stronger flow
my being follows the flow
now ten beats to a movement slow
soft beats to a song rift below

*

then a sharp pain breath
a breath of life in
my heartbeats seven times
a breath of life flying out
floating in the air flow
my eyes open to a sound
lips close around a word on a breath
jesus my jesus is heard
am i jesus
am i alive
seven heartbeats in breath
seven heartbeats out breath

*

in the beginning
my mother whispered my name jesus
this name is what it will prove to be
how close to god it will become
measured by these words in your mind
these words are the creator
heaven and earth may pass away
the creator words will live forever
follow the way in
to be with the creator forever
look to the stars
see the north star
circled by the chariot of heaven

the constant star
follow the wagon of heaven
the plow of heaven
you are the earth being plowed
furrows turning in the heavens
the pointer stars show the way in
the centre star the door inside
the centre spindle creating a spool
a spool of life
the yarn your life
this story wrapped around the star of the way in
your being is the way in
the light path mind and soul
the words created by the alpha and the omega
known by some as jah
known by all as the supreme god
god above all other gods   all jah
*

let your being find all jah
the centre light as you circle in time
the thunder in clouds claps time
you are a raindrop in time
you are a raindrop falling
one life one drop
from the cloud to the sea
time is one drop
a falling raindrop of your life
formed falling then fading
into the sea
one lifetime one drop
*

my mother mary held me in her arms
as a babe unaware of all but her
my mother sheltered me as a son of angels
asleep and content with the stars circling around me
my body wrapped in a golden white glow
wrapped in love with mother
glowing light like heartbeats
each beat a day long

seven days glowing
*

then rough hands took me
bar joseph words
brit milah circumcision
day and night pain there
fear and crying
why did you let them cut me
why mother mary
*

she held my little hand
the rain of time in one moment
as we walked along the seashore on the sand
as we strolled along the seashore on the beach
a rainbow appeared
there i awoke to the glory of god
in that raindrop of time
the yellow sun shining bright in the blue sky of my eyes
my eyes are the twinkling flash on small waves on the blue sea
the blue green sea of love my turquoise color
the rainbow of awakening
past clouds cleared
jah showed the world
opened in time to me
my future a full life to be
whispered in the wind
life in the wind opened to love
awakened to the glory of life to be lived
holding my mothers hand
as we strolled along the seashore on the sand
*

in alexandria
there i was a boy playing
at the feet of mothers
mothers who shared a village
speaking many languages
all the children playing together
we learned to speak many languages
languages learned

at the feet of mothers who shared a village
a new language learned every year
by the age of six my languages counted six tongues
all at the feet of mothers in alexandria
mothers who worked together making papyrus
papyrus for scrolls for the library
scrolls for scribes to use creating scripts
all words numbers in order and harmony
sounds make languages as music
words are notes of music to be played
at the feet of mothers in alexandria
*

papa joseph took me to the harbor
he worked as a carpenter building ships
this is how we make it strong
use thick wood for ribs and planks
fill the cracks with pitch to seal it long
creating a boat we give god thanks
through us a female vessel will belong
as a helper to men on the sea
papa joseph taught the way to me
that a carpenter creates ships
*

a yellow dog followed me home
a scrappy and happy stray dog
soft eyes asked for a home
eager eyes colored yellow
his name became saffron
spice in my life
saffron gave lessons on how to smell
how to really use my nose
this meat this bread this road dust
smell each fish each pomegranate each fig
smell each flower each mother
saffron the king of smell
also taught me how to think like a dog
how to listen every morning
how to protect our flock
of children

how to look out for others
learning lessons from dog
from men as teachers too
a master of the library in alexandria
a master of the mothers in the papyrus shop
a teacher named david became my master
david taught me about words
scrolls written in different languages
stories of old in words on scrolls
messages from men of old to guide
seekers of wisdom
jesus now a seeker of wisdom
saffron spice at my side
*

the way of david was to teach with fables
words of aesop about the raven dropping rocks
into a jar to raise the water level to drink
wisdom
to care about beauty and form
the word song of solomon the lover
aristophanes tickled bellies
when his frogs croaked
laughter
let us tickle the world
words of euripedes
words of the trojan women
voices to the people of the cities
stories of homer
stories sang songs
odysseus the hero of voyages
*

there are scrolls of histories
abraham
deeds of men
heros of endless wars
alexander to augustus
scrolls of sacred and solemn states
worship and prayers to gods
homages to holy heros

inspirations and instructions
the great pharaoh tombs to enter the afterlife
the law words for moses
on stone tablets
tablets of jah
kept in a box
the ark the boat
the ark now gone
the boat sailed on
no scroll told where
*

rabbi david was a roman citizen
david a roman jew
master of words
daylight days were under his skies
guided by his staff
nose sniffing out scrolls
the scrolls of alexandria
at the delta of the great river
flowed knowledge of the world
the world of words flowed
as the nile through the desert
*

saffron stayed at my feet smelling the skies
signaling snakes among the scrolls
slithering slaughter for rats
rats are the enemy of codex and scroll
rats chew the edges and snakes chew the rats
snakes and cats are allies in a war on rats
sometimes snakes turned on cats
saffron was on the side of cats
he would sniff out snakes and take a cat killers life
snakes can be a danger to men as well
seekers of wisdom must avoid snakes
our duty was to know where each snake was sliding
protect the cats and the people from bites
*

the library had many buildings and many rooms
some were filled with shelves of scrolls and codex books

some had benches for meetings of scholars
some were for lectures by teachers
some rooms had tables to read books and scrolls
writings of words fetched by clerks of the library
myself a clerk finding lumps of letters

*

one day my brother james was with me
listening to me revealing wisdom in a scroll
my name was called from another room by a clerk
saffron came with me to help him
suddenly there was a scream from james
left behind in the room
he was bitten
saffron snapped the snake
he tossed it like a whip
to death
as if he was a wolf
my knife cut open
the bite marks on james
to suck out the poison
spit it on the ground
medicine was calling to me
use what is in the scrolls
ways to save the stricken
herbs and remedies from healing words
suck out the poison to save him
my destiny
jesus the savior
beginning with my brother james

*

rabbi david said the rats are possessed
they seek out the most precious scrolls
especially anything that is about jah
how could rats know what is in a codex
the devil must be in them directing them
chew here gnaw this destroy gods words
after observing the truth of the destruction
my reaction was to trap six rats
keep them alive in an empty store room

study them try to read their minds
they had a squeak language
certain signals and smelling ways
one was a leader over the others
the king
eating his fill first of the grain given them
establishing his throne at a straw perch in a corner
keeping both females as his wives
the other three males each took a corner
but only the ruler went wherever he wished
if the rats were possessed then he was a master
yet there was no way into his mind
no key for me to learn what was inside no key
whatever controlled their thoughts was a mystery
rabbi david saw satan in them
a rat possession mystery

II

at age nine my family returned to judea
without me
mother and father
three brothers two sisters all left
left alone with rabbi david
alone with saffron
walking on the beach alone
the grains of sand like stars
each grain a world in the palm of my hand
a dove flew onto my shoulder and sang
a haunted song to soothe my lonely heart
the honey from the bees comb enters my body
echoes of the dove song enter the hive inside me
there is the smell of the flowers the bees visited
the flowers the sheep ate the soft smell
a lamb asks where his mother went
mother sheep stomps her hoof
tells lamb to come
but no one stamps for me
high in the air an eagle sees the fish in the sea
from heaven it dives into the sea
takes the fish and drops it to me
jah will take care of me
walking on the beach alone
on a path of moonlight
*

avoid the thorn bushes on the beach of words
at the age of ten there were more languages
student friends to debate the scrolls
aristotle says the sun around the earth
aristarchus says the world around the sun
more sense from aristarchus
rabbi david showed us the stars
the belt of orion
sirius the dog star

the wandering stars were planets
and above all the north star polaris
my personal star
every person has a star of their own
or one to share with others
boys and girls each with their own star
and their own tongue to taste the heavens
each had a separate smell aroused by their voices
each student a unique smell sometimes sweet sometimes sour
like a taste for each dish yet a smell like a color
a separate color for each as a halo
one green reminding me of oregano
several with shades of brown like pepper or cloves
yellow brown color in one like cinnamon
others colored like ripe red raspberries
some smelling and looking like a blue sage sky
each student had a unique color and smell
each a memory of thought colors fragrances
each their own language words
each a favorite saying to debate me
colors delight debate in musical rhythm
the way in through different languages
weaving through the thorny smells
avoiding thorn bushes on the beach of words

*

eyes signal more than smell and colors
eyes are you alone on the beach of sand
a hole of black surrounded by a matchless pattern
some eyes have a starburst pattern within a color
others a dark circle within another colored circle
some eyes have patterns of dots and specks
every persons eyes are unlike every other individual
colors abound from black and grey to brown and gold
green and amber, blue as the sky blue as the sea
yellow circles even rare purple many shades
myriad combinations of colors and patterns
the eyes are truly doors to the origin of that person

*

this is a holy ritual of the way in
the way in through the eyes

stand in the sunlight facing your friend
reach out and gently hold each others hands
stand and look into the others eyes
look intently into that window
see the color within their eyes
let images in the eyes patterns form pictures
smell the pictures colors of places
as you let the pictures of your own eyes shine out
the energy of the love within you reaches out
allows you to feel the others energy
glowing all around that person and into your eyes
this is the exchange of visions
a holy ritual of eyes embracing
imagined pictures trading colors
you see my pictures and i see yours
a holy ritual of the way in

*

at eleven years old rabbi david took me
to study how doctors worked
to study secret healing arts
this doctor could bind broken limbs
cut out growths and sew together cut flesh
that doctor gave potions and medicines
others persuaded with soothing words
some commanded illness to leave the inside
cast out the sickness like demons
make way for health to come in
the words opening the way in
to have the eyes of the other made whole
the eyes made clear again

*

later that year my father sailed into port
joseph had built a small trading ship
with a crew of four to sail it
his cargo was olive oil for alexandria
picking up a load of papyrus paper for crete
my brother james and cousin lazarus
born close in age to me
were also with papa joseph
my father asked me to come also to crete

where he was to pick up wine for a return trip
david gave permission on the condition
that I investigate the ruins at knossos
it was amusing to play games with the boys on board
wrestling each other
trying out tricks that were in a codex i had read
at the old palace on crete
frescos on walls brought the ancients to life
acrobats jumping over bulls
also floor mosaics of frolicking with dolphins
pictures of musical instruments came to life
as we made up songs imagining the music
we walked the ruins of the labyrinth
following the advice princess ariadne gave theseus
straight ahead never turning left or right
always going downward
there at the centre I pretended to be the minotaur
king minos in a bull mask
challenging lazarus as theseus to a wrestling match
james swooned this way and that as the princess
stop she said king minos cannot win
when I had pinned lazarus down
theseus is the hero
we can change stories i said
ancient myths are not reality
in this story the minotaur wins

*

on the return voyage
my father sang sailors songs
he taught us the tunes of a saga of theseus
the six labors of the greek hero
first beat the clubber bandit by wrestling his staff away
in the second labor against sinis
turn the tables on the pine tree robber
sinis was himself tied to two pine trees
that had been bent to the ground
when theseus released the trees sinis was torn apart
then he took the daughter perigune as a slave
a woman to fondle as he pleased

a woman to help him in his third task
to defeat the giant sow demon
the old crone phaea turned herself into a pig
theseus was stronger than the giant sow
he wrestled her to the ground
his slave girl perigune bound the feet
they roasted the pig over a fire
a very tasty old crone sow theseus said
fourth he faced the tricky old robber sciron
if you want to use my path along the cliff face
you must first wash my feet to pay the toll
perigune warned theseus beforehand
sciron kicks travellers off the cliff
to feed the sea monsters below
theseus took hold of the ankles
tossed sciron off the cliff
the fifth labor was made for theseus
king cercyon challenged passersby
to a wrestling match with the loser beheaded
no one could beat mighty theseus in wrestling
the sharp sword of theseus dispatched
the king of the bandits
yet there was one dangerous old bandit left
a sixth labor against a trickster
a man called procrustes the stretcher
he offered travellers the choice of one of two guest beds
one bed very short and the other very long
if you chose the short bed
he would chop off your feet while you slept
just making you fit better he would say
if you chose the long bed when you fell asleep
he would tie your ankles and wrists
and stretch you to make you fit
no body completed a nights sleep in his guest beds
every body was made to fit
yet perigune fit the short bed perfectly
theseus was very tall and fit the long bed truly
procrustes insisted that the two switch beds
theseus said no let us fit you in instead

first stretching procrustes on the long bed
then chopping off his feet and his head
to fit the short bed
that was the tale of the six labors
a saga song of theseus the hero
*

dolphins were leaping beside the boat on the way back
they were calling out and i was echoing their voices
papa joseph said that i should learn to talk with them
they can be wonderful friends
lazarus said he would rather ride them than talk
back in alexandria
my father said farewell to me
first joining me in my holy ritual eye vision exchange
his eyes were kind dark honey balls with slivers of cinnamon
sweet smells at an oasis in the desert
*

at the library three men came
who claimed to know my father
a slippery looking oil merchant named joshua
along with his friends a blacksmith and a baker
claimed to want to borrow some books
they asked me to show them the best scrolls
it was clear to me that they could not read
their eyes inner colors could be read
here is a very valuable scroll for the blacksmith
a picture book with drawings of tools
look here baker a very valuable scroll
a book of manners at the table
here is a scroll for you oil man
a dump of a fire bucket of water over your head
saffron drove them out
the wet one joshua cursing me
a call to chase them out the door
your plans were read by the tools in my mind
mind your manners at the meal of learning
watch out for the rain that washes you out
here at the library you may get what you need

more likely what you deserve
knowledge is to learn not to steal
*

at twelve there was a trip to jerusalem
to be with mother and family again
mary and joseph james jude simon ruth and hanna
josephs sister anna and her son lazarus
all joined me at the temple
listening to the rabbis debates
which i joined in sharing some words of the scrolls
wise words that i had memorized
to the priests riddles answers flowed
answers to questions of the temple
jewish customs the law and jah
from my readings and the wisdom of the way in
they accepted the love of my eyes
even when they looked away
their colors were open
the inside was revealed
their unique place on the earth revealed
the condition of their state of being
within the love of jah
*

joseph warned me beware of the yeast
of the words of the sadducees
the yeast is hypocrisy hidden in the bread from their words
when they questioned me there was no fear
they tried to find yeast in my words
this is what they know
hidden meanings hidden rules
my rule was to speak truth
from my inner rooms
**whatever you have said in darkness
will be heard in light I told them
there is nothing covered up
that will not be revealed
there is nothing hidden
that will not be known**
*

all the family returned to nazareth
only lazarus came back with me to alexandria
lazarus went to school with me
enrolled with rabbi david
first lesson for lazarus was to work in the stables
caring for horses stallions to love
lessons from the medicine scrolls
lazarus made medicines from plants
good for horses good for men
we began to ride horses as well as clean after them
in the stables lazarus told me of his childhood
his father had died before he was born
another man married his mother anna
fathered two sisters and then he too died
how did he die I asked
murdered by zealots as a collaborator with romans
he denied it but there must have been some truth
how did you learn about that
some roman strangers came to the house
every month inquiring how i was growing
leaving bags of money for my health and education
lots of money for family expenses they said
our neighbors thought my mother anna was a harlot
shunned her for her contact with romans
she was no harlot it was all on account of me
is that why she sent you to alexandria
she asked the romans for permission first
anna told me that a jewish merchant had proposed marriage
but I had to be sent away first
my true father was a roman distaining to be step father to me
he knew that as a virgin my mother had been sold by her father
to romans and taken to their temple
fed wine suffered the lust of a roman
then sent back to her parents carrying me inside
but because she was beautiful she was again sold
to an old jewish merchant as his slave wife
the old merchant was father to my sisters
why did your roman father not keep your mother as his slave
she told me that he was married to a very jealous roman wife
it was easier for him to have his men keep an eye on me

who is your roman father
one of his men let it slip that he was a general
they encouraged me to become a warrior for rome
but i promised my mother i would not be a soldier
so I am in alexandria to find something else
find your destiny in the barns i joked
maybe if i learn to whisper the language of horses

*

we did learn to understand horses together
two horses owned by a roman patron of the library
two stallions became our instructors
my stallion named golden eyes
golden brown color with lighter mane and tail
the other a black stallion for lazarus
laughingly called lucifer
black light footed lucifer
lazarus eyes the same color as his stallions
lazarus eyes like shadows
dark as the god of light
secret eyes of a mystery father
at dawn we rode along the seashore
dashing in and out of the surf
pounding the sand racing to win
the pinnacle rock at the end of the beach
my horses golden eyes
blow kindness
the eyes of lazarus flashed
just like his stallions
light in the shadows of lucifers eyes
secrets of the shadows
lazarus and lucifer
who is this dark shadow my friend
the lonely self beside me
who is his real father i wondered
as we rode back to the stables
two friends on horseback
was lazarus a roman cowbird
a chick from an egg laid in a songbirds nest

*

at times we worked at the shipyards
eating our lunch on the dock
swimming in the ocean
resting there to watch the dolphins and listen
to the high pitched tweets and tickles
calling to one in its language
it responding with songs at hearing me
all the words of dolphins are songs
learning to speak with them was slow
yet they are eager to teach if you really listen
they speak too fast and too high to easily grasp
you must keep trying
to sing the songs to speak with dolphins
into the water and they read our hearts
into the water and they see into our minds
into the water and they swim with us
rewards for me and lazarus
we rode dolphins as horses of the sea
my ears heard the high notes of dolphin words
lazarus did not try to speak dolphin language
he felt it pass through him
content to let his body listen instead
he understood the horse language
he knew some of the dog language
a few words of the other student languages
lazarus was learning from life more than books
while the music and language that embraced me
my ease with languages from my time with the mothers
workshop blessings and gifts
enabled dolphin talk
with words from the dolphins a way of seeing
with my eyes closed my tongue clicking like them
walking blind in the dark i could see
by listening to the echoes of my clicks
bounced back to me from walls corners trees
other people walking or sitting down
this click bounce gift i taught to a blind man
a beggar on the steps of the library
as he learned i opened my own eyes
saw the color from him turn golden white with joy

a blind man learned to see by listening the dolphin way
lazarus also learned this way of listening
we created miracles of teaching the blind to see
*

to rabbi david i said
can the blind guide the blind
would they not both fall into a pit
the teacher you follow should see clearly
even if he is blind he may see with his ears
and avoid the pit
*

there are other ways to see
other ways to hear
the language of emotion came as color
not just when greeting friends
greetings exchanging colors in holy ritual
eyes closed color from inside for each emotion
anger is fire red and brimstone black
love is azure sea
a full belly is green
pasture grass
a passion is lapis luce
robes to enfold you
a love for all is golden white
radiant marble sunlight
each emotion has a color in this language
like notes of music
like dolphin words
meet each person
see the color within each person
the color of the way in
read your own color of emotion within
the scrolls are words left behind
footprints fading in the sand gone grey
but the colors come new with each emotion
each other person has a resting color
a music note that other colors come out of
as a light from a lamp through their eyes
the color in the eyes
specific to each person

the color in the eyes tells of a special place
a distinct place in the world
in one persons eyes
fresh plowed earth in eqypt
in anothers eyes
a peach tree with grass around
when i look into the way in through anothers eyes
the place where they are marked from on the earth
the color of the eyes matches the root of the person
revealed in the ritual of visionary insights
what can be seen from the edge
of the way in
awareness of awareness
in a mirror my own eyes kissed each other
the blue of the sea with a star flash at the centre
*

a roman centurion marcellus
met with rabbi david and asked for me
he wanted me to teach my languages and music
to his two children
a boy rufus aged six
a girl penelope aged eight
two gifted children to instruct
penelope with a voice from high up
a singer born like a song bird
rufus the builder the architect
hands wanting to shape clay or wood
these two learned greek language
they learned greek culture and history
alexander the great founded the city
our city alexandria a centre for learning
a life for them to grow in creation
a celebration of greek culture
a great lighthouse to shine in the fog of the minds of men
a beacon to show the way in
we climbed to the top of the great lighthouse
searched the horizon for distant ships
the world is a globe a ball i showed them
when a distant ship gets closer
first you see the top of sails then the whole boat

see this speck on this ball
as it rolls towards me i see it
the earth is like this round ball
there is much science to learn
as well as culture and religion
the greek gods rule the temples
now with roman names i taught them
jupiter is zeus the god of gods
jupiters wife is juno the greek hera
mars the god of war like ares
mercury the gods messenger like hermes
poseidon is now the roman neptune god of the sea
dionysus has become bacchus god of wine and revels
eros the god of love is now cupid
similar stories in different languages
different words for the same things
mimic my words penelope
memorize the names rufus
many gods and many more from egypt
they were instructed about their stories
knowledge but avoid beliefs in their gods
in my hebrew language the prophets teach
there is only one true god the creator
the language of jah is told in stories of people
people who struggle to learn
learn the true creative words of jahs worshippers
in the scrolls in hebrew language
marcellus said no to hebrew
teach them greek stories of wonder
heroes and demigods and mortal men
teach the twelve labors of hercules
theseus battling the amazons
how jason was taught by the centaur chiron
the voyage of jason and the argonauts
remember medea luring the snake to sleep
allowing jason to capture the golden fleece
teach rufus about perseus beheading medusa
daedalus creating wings for icarus too
it would be wonderful to fly as a bird
young rufus shouted

penelope wanted to know more stories too
paris and helen and the war at troy
achilles and hector and the trojan horse
yes rufus said excited my favorite greek tale
my favorite is from the poet homer i told them
most exciting of all is odysseus wandering
eating the lotus fruit and forgetting
escaping the cyclops under the belly of a ram
the strong winds of aeolus let out of the bag
circe the sorceress turning his men into pigs
the descent into the underworld
sailing past the sirens past scylla and charybdis
losing his men after they ate the oxen of the sun
loving calypso for years until she released him
told odysseus the way home
follow the pointer stars
hold them on your heart side
the wain the great bear on your heart side
the way home again to ithaca and loyal penelope
my name too the young penelope sighed
*

only some old masters at the library took disciples
young scholars who were eager to learn
one old master taught musical instruments
penelope followed me in his classes
there was another girl with a loving laugh
sara shared her figs for lunch
traded me for some of my fish
she shared funny fits of laughter
the joy of all the small things she saw
pure water was sweet from her cup
the smile of sara captured my mind
young penelope reminded me sternly
sara has been promised to another
all she has for you is a warm wind
blossoms of apricots
as sara played the kitara
her right hand with a plectrum plucking petals
her left hand catching each falling note drop
the perfect echo of the turtle shell body

cat gut strings whined high notes
purring strings gave low notes
parts of cats brought to life again in her hands
her love of them confirmed with her pet cat cleo
always following sara rubbing against her
sara showed us all how to really play the lyre
the seven stringed lyre called the kitara
from sara to the dolphins the music flowed
my dolphin friends teased me
imitating saras laughter
saffron wagged his tail and blew away the blossoms
only great golden eye let me listen
to the power of his heartbeat
the power of his eyes reaching deep
on his back his dancing hooves held the beat
as the kitara spoke to the dolphins
as my kitara sang copies of sara
she then shared another gift
how to listen to cats in their language
how to purr growl spit tail curl
blink ear flick and all the body moves
that all cats use to communicate
translated in her playing the kitara
*

at a feast sara performed
after lilies were handed out and the beer flowed
between the roast duck with garlic and coriander
and the pie of papyrus roots with dates and figs
sara mocked the egyptian gods in a song
saras song
*

flow river flow flow nile flow
seth the pig rules the river
when the river floods you turn into hapi
hapi the flood god hapi seth the pig
flow hapi flow flow seth flow
baal the sky god is missing from above
the sky goddess nut is missing too
there are no nuts and baals falling from the sky
sobek the crocodile ate them

flow river flow flow sobek flow
hathor the cow dances on the riverbank
babi the baboon wants to mate with her
baboons mate with cows and laugh
jump and hump on the banks of the nile
flow river flow flow babi flow
buchis the bull is chased by the lioness
sekhmet licks her lips at buchis
but the bull tosses her into the river
thoth the moon god looks down on them
flow moon flow flow nile flow
the falcon horus bites the cobra wadjet
the horus beak murders the wadjet fangs
more murder as osiris the father is set upon by set
set the chaos god is the new ruler
flow chaos flow flow river flow
mother isis misses father osiris
she brings osiris back from the dead
he walks again under the sun god ra
ra turns the river into beer
flow beer flow flow beer flow
overflow
*

the crowd laughed
the crowd drank the beer
saras father scowled
he would not allow her to sing again
never offend the egyptian people
never mock their gods sara
this made me see red brimstone
why not mock the false gods
do not bite the hand that feeds
saras father took her away from the library
she left me her now forbidden song
her gift of playing the kitara passed to me
to mock the false gods for her
*

marcellus took his family sailing
i sang to the dolphins on the prow of the ship
they sang back echoes of the song of sara

two years teaching rufus and penelope
in teaching i was taught first by penelope
who had learned from sara how to talk with cleo the cat
messages were sent with cleo to sara
then i was taught how to draw by rufus
lines and forms and shadows
we learned to paint frescos together
filling rooms with picture stories
mocking the egyptian gods

*

marcellus added to the knowledge from my father
he taught me how to sail even in slack wind
the current is a friend not a foe
on a trip up the nile to thebes
he allowed lazarus to come as well
a slow peaceful journey up the mighty nile
marcellus on a mission
to welcome the queen of nubia
into the roman world as a new servant
lessons in diplomacy
lessons of egyptian monuments
lessons in sailing on mighty waters
first we stopped at the great pyramids
these mighty mountains made by men
pharaohs made these three pyramids
into the stars of orions belt
pharaohs were the incarnations of those stars
pyramids on earth to match the stars
their heavenly homes are death holes lazarus quipped
on we sailed to luxor temple in thebes
huge statues of ramses at its gates
tall pylons obelisks covered in writing
the luxor temple built in three curves
curves like the body of a man
a temple of man to honor the god amun
amun was the creator god
amun was the egyptian jah
not a ruler like jupiter or zeus
a creator god like jah
next we went to dendera

to the newly built roman temple there
the walls full of carvings of roman emperors
side by side with old egyptian pharaohs
the temple dedicated to the goddess hathor
wife of the falcon god horus
inside the temple in a roof chapel dedicated to osiris
there was a sundial and a zodiac
the zodiac had two centres
one center was my true north star
the star polaris the centre of the heavens
outside of this temple marcellus met a procession
the queen of the nubians paying homage
to the roman gods ruling the world
augustus and his representative marcellus
lazarus admired her beautiful black skin
whispered to me that he would like to rub it
like his horse lucifers nose
his eyes desired more of her than her eyes
lazarus looked lustfully long at her legs
back down the nile we floated
animals birds crocodiles along the shore
everything transformed into gods
a thousand egyptian gods
lazarus and i wrestled together on deck
he was taller and stronger
i was quick and full of fast tricks
using mind moves fast holds pressure points
always surprising my opponents
*

marcellus revealed a secret to me
there was a high roman official interested in me
someone he gave reports to
was he the same man who favored lazarus i asked
no he laughed and laughed again
all the way back to alexandria
just because you call yourself jesus bar joseph
does not mean joseph is your real father
just because your phallus is mutilated
does not mean you are a jew
the loudest laughter then at lazarus

if i cut my foreskin off am i your father
perhaps lazarus said but i have read
the ancient egyptians
had that practice before the jews
it keeps the penis from infections
it also tightens the pleasure head
maybe my father was an egyptian
the only pleasure jews ever got from egyptians
was the whip marcellus refuted
what do you think jesus he asked
**the marking of a penis is egyptian tradition
moses should have left it behind there
it is left over superstition
the cutting means nothing to me**

*

III

rabbi david prepared lazarus and i
for our bar mitzvah at age thirteen
we were to become sons of the law
full members of the tribes and assembly
if we accepted the laws of the jews
yet the tradition of questioning the traditions
led us to wrestle with each law
which laws were acceptable to us for our times
which laws were old relics that were better history
*

my bar mitzvah wrestling began
THE FIRST OLD COMMANDMENT IS
DO NOT WORSHIP ANY OTHER GODS
DO NOT HAVE ANY OTHER GODS BEFORE ME
the first commandment that i accept is
jehovah the creator is all the air all the earth
all the sea all the sun the moon and the stars
all the things you see outside yourself
yet you can bring jehovah inside yourself
love the creator with your whole heart
with your whole soul your whole being
become one with the creator inside the me
*

THE SECOND OLD LAW WAS
DO NOT WORSHIP IDOLS
DO NOT MAKE IMAGES TO WORSHIP
DO NOT COPY ANYTHING IN CREATION
DO NOT BOW DOWN NOR SERVE THEM
JAH BRINGS PUNISHMENT FOR THIS TRANSGRESSION
ONTO THE FAMILY OF THE TRANSGRESSOR
PUNISHMENT DOWN TO THE FOURTH GENERATION
little images are to laugh about i said
in worshipping the only god jehovah
beside you he will laugh at idols
there is joy with laughter not punishment
laughter at you down to the fourth generation

if you are a fool to worship idols

*

THE THIRD OLD LAW WAS
DO NOT TAKE THE NAME OF JEHOVAH IN VAIN
DO NOT USE JAH IN A WORTHLESS WAY
JAH WILL PUNISH ANY WHO DISOBEY
my law is there is only one god
i am what i will prove to be
the meaning of the name jehovah
i am what i will prove to be
is not a name that is sacred
it is the being behind the name
that no curse can touch
jehovah fears no curses
cursing laws are outdated
rabbi david scolded me
just agree never to mock jehovah

*

THE FOURTH OLD LAW IS
DO NOT FORGET THE SABBATH
DO NO WORK ON THE SABBATH
DO NOT ALLOW YOUR FAMILY TO WORK
DO NOT ALLOW YOUR SERVANTS NOR GUESTS TO WORK
JAH CREATED EVERYTHING IN SIX DAYS
ON THE SEVENTH HE CHOSE TO REST
THIS IS THE COMMANDMENT THAT YOU DO AS HE DID
my fourth law is sharing my time every day
in praying and reflecting on jahs work
my work also having jah at rest inside me
every day is thus a sabbath day
lazarus agreed with what i said
if your brother has anything against you
leave rest on any day and go to him
first be reconciled with your brother
then have a day of rest from your creation
rabbi david said who can argue

*

THE FIFTH OLD LAW WAS
DO NOT DISHONOR YOUR MOTHER NOR FATHER
DO NOT SHORTEN YOUR DAYS WITH DISRESPECT

my new law goes farther
jehovah is the creator of your father and mother
love the vessels that carried you to your existence
share in creation honor yourself as a creator
honor yourself as a mother and a father
honor your children and they will honor you
bless those who curse you
even if your parents disown you
jah above lets the sun shine on the just
as well as the sun shine on the unjust
jah above is your father and mother
very good rabbi david said
*

THE SIXTH OLD LAW IS DO NOT MURDER
DO NOT KILL ANOTHER PERSON
my word is those deserving of death are in jahs hands
jehovah is a creator of life a lover of life
inside yourself create and love life
when you are with jah there is no time for death
there is no room for a killer in his palace
creating murder will keep you outside
let your life be as a creator rather than a destroyer
lazarus agreed that we must stay away from war
carry no weapons and speak only forgiveness
then you agree not to murder
the rabbi concluded
more than that i say
everyone who is angry with his brother
has thoughts of murder in his heart
learn to laugh at your anger
if anyone strikes your right cheek
let him strike your left cheek also
you love your friends naturally
love your enemies more than friends
let your thoughts be good will to all
*

THE SEVENTH OLD LAW IS DO NOT COMMIT ADULTERY
DO NOT FORNICATE WITH ANOTHER PERSON
IF EITHER OF YOU ARE BOUND IN MARRIAGE

in the law rabbi david offered
jehovah respects men and women equally
the two as one are blessed in union
having any sex outside of a marriage dishonors jah
should the law be against rape
against forced sex lazarus asked
is sex with slaves adultery
is sex with paid prostitutes permissible
the rabbi said it is cloudy there
you do not commit adultery unless you are married
lazarus concluded the law should be against lust
regardless of marriage
rabbi david insisted you young men will have to accept
this law before you can marry
then leave it until then i said
my interpretation that i commit to is
if you love someone in your heart
wait until your hearts are married to each other
before you have a marriage ceremony
otherwise openly face your creator alone
on the way in be true to your heart
adultery is empty sex without your heart
it is worship to a false god

*

THE EIGHTH OLD LAW IS DO NOT STEAL
DO NOT TAKE WHAT BELONGS TO ANOTHER
my new eighth law is give instead of taking
give all that you have to others freely
let others give to you freely
let giving be a way in to jah
if anyone asks you to go a mile go two
if anyone wants your coat give it to him
my eighth law is give all your material goods away
less goods means less worry over material things
more time to do the will of jah
*
THE NINTH LAW IS DO NOT BEAR FALSE WITNESS
DO NOT LIE ABOUT ANOTHER PERSON
my new law is truth telling is the way to jah

false truths are stumbling blocks on the way
let your yes be yes and your no be no
leave swearing by jah or your own head
as stones along the path of the way in
judge not that you will not be judged
very good the rabbi said
*

THE TENTH LAW IS DO NOT COVET ANOTHERS HOUSE
DO NOT COVET ANOTHERS MARRIAGE PARTNER
DO NOT COVET ANOTHERS WORKERS NOR LIVELIHOOD
NOR ANYTHING THAT BELONGS TO ANOTHER
my new tenth law is let all the beings
all the people and possessions in your heart
all the things you desire all your old gods
be set aside as time distraction
on the path of the way to jah
lay up treasures in heaven
those on the earth are passing away
you cannot serve both mammon and jah
who of you who is anxious for things of the earth
can add one moment of life i ask
who can trade their things for more time on earth
the tenth law is to follow the better path
towards time with the invisible spirit of jah
amen said the rabbi
*

with our own understanding
our own wrestling
what the laws are about
until we wrestle with scripture
we do not know it
was the wrestling of jacob with an angel
a way in to touch the truth
or just a sport that even jah enjoys
so it was that lazarus and i became
confirmed sons of the laws of jehovah
confirmed wrestlers of scripture
*

IV

marcellus saw us ride along the beach
my golden back on golden eye above the sea surf
lazarus was lucifer leaping over waves
marcellus had ambition for his chariots
an olympic horse team driven by us
holding reins in chariots
he saw us behind the team
dark lazarus and lucifer
joyful jesus and golden eye
the horses opened their minds to me
accepted the seeds of victory
mind instructions to win
at age fifteen we were princes of the chariot
every race we entered
laurels for marcellus

*

marcellus sailed with us to greece
to compete in the olympic games
lazarus the driver behind our two stallions
myself in the wrestling competitions
there at olympia we trained in the gymnasium
also at the stadium behind the horses
holding golden eyes reins and whispering to his heart
the power to run pulling from heaven
lucifer laughed in joy and power touched by lazarus
lazarus in the chariot
jesus toppling the wrestling gods
winning ways in champions
laurel crowns for us as olympic champions
the one hundred and ninety eighth olympiad
we won for our patron marcellus
he owned the horses and collected on his bets
marcellus poured wine until we fell
on our faces too drunk to stand
we woke bewildered and nude

in the temple to zeus
standing ten times the height of a man
gilded and covered in precious stones
the statue loomed over us
our vomit at his feet
looking up at the huge statue of the god
a wonder of the world
we could not stop laughing
a priest gave us a bucket
to clean up
under the giant idol
for days the festival rang our praises
with the revelers and bacchus
too staggered to stand anymore celebrations
too naked
we finally found clothes
then ran off
to explore the lands of greece

*

lazarus was interested in the healer god asclepius
father of hippocrates with the power to raise the dead
we went to a temple spa where the sick congregated
the healing was body and soul
athletics baths theatre dance and song
singing at the perfect sound echoing theatre
a whisper from the centre point stage
heard clearly from the distant back row
after days with the doctors we left
journeyed to delphi to unwind the times
understand prophecy and the future
we washed our sins away first at a spring
sprung in the footprints of pegasus
then went to the temple of the god apollo
apollo god of bright sunshine music and prophecy
the priestess there was possessed by him and spoke
the oracle knew us as soon as our eyes embraced
greetings jesus and lazarus
lazarus you will find the medicine from asclepius
the potions to raise the dead back to life
you will need it for yourself one day

you will need it for your loved ones too
you will have great adventures ahead
jesus play your kitara for me please
you are the son of a god to be
and you will become a god even greater
a god grown out of a man mortal no more
you will be known as a healer and teacher
an anointed prophet a messiah
first you must learn the wisdom of the world
hear the words of the old masters
become a prince of peace and love
a king of the jews
a savior for your people
the oracle listened as my kitara
sang my future with the notes
humming a song for her ears
the oracle fell silent
*

the oracle did not foreshadow a calamity
my bold saffron took sick and lay still
the ministrations of lazarus would not raise him
his mind would not respond to mine
saffron the snake killer was old
saffron passed the color in his eyes to me
yellow gold
saffron lay cold
i howled as a wolf for him
*

the chariot triumph in greece
led to a voyage to rome
more people than in any other city
rome more famed than babylon
rome famed as the centre of the world
there at the centre of rome augustus ruled
the princeps the emperor of the world
proclaiming himself its god
marcellus had us entered in a race
a circus maximus five chariot challenge
battle of the best
hosted by tiberius the heir of augustus

winner of the one hundred ninety fourth olympics
in his youth a triumphant warrior hero
still formidable in the race himself
it began with lazarus holding second to a very quick team
tiberius at the back biding his time
the fastest will tire out
round and round
first one team pacing the chariot of lazarus harassing him
then another team trying to trip his horses with wheels
the lead team slowed
two teams flanked lazarus
all four teams drifted to the outside
as tiberius passed them all along the inside
laurels to him posing before the princeps in the stands
marcellus presented lucifer and golden eyes as gifts
to the pater patriae father of the country of rome
marcellus owned our horses we had no say
over the tears in our eyes as we said goodbye to each
our stallions torn away as lost bets to augustus
gifts at the altar of caesar

*

augustus summoned me to his palace
an audience with the princeps is an honor marcellus said
our caesar augustus will be named a god when he dies
following in the footsteps of the god julius caesar
what a privilege he wants to watch you in private
wrestling against his favorite

*

arriving at his villa an hour after sunset
augustus invited me to lounge on a couch
listen to some singers watch dancers
the table set for a feast
would you play the kitara for me he asked
as a slave brought one to me and i obliged
next the very civil discourse
questions he already knew answers to from his spies
all about my family my father joseph
deep interest in my mother mary
he knew her name without being told
asked about her health her well being

her emotional being
he ate simple bread figs dates and grapes
nibbling lightly as the time rolled by
then how i enjoyed rabbi david the famous scholar
my trips to crete and up the nile
ancient greek philosophers
the poet homer
had i read virgil
his favorite book the aeneid
yes the story of the origins of romans and his family
the julian ancestors
aenius was more human than odysseus
less arrogant and selfish than achilles
even when he is confused afraid or despondent
he could inspire his men
aeneas respected his father augustus commented
temptation by queen dido of carthage was put aside
for the good of rome
the death of turnus in the end
cleopatra is not given honor in the book
she was past her prime when i saw her die augustus said
her son caesarian was about your age when he died
he was one i regret losing
silence
the loss of julius caesars son was a blow to our line
yet had he lived it would have been civil war
silence and he fell asleep for a while
waking suddenly
time for you to wrestle my man marcus
come out you long haired gaul he ordered
we stripped naked
marcus was shorter than me and stocky
there is no time limit on a bout
winning was pinning an opponents shoulder to the ground
and holding to the count of three by augustus
no attacking the groin poking eyes or biting
standing face to face with marcus
we grasped each other and grappled
trying to swing or trip the other down
looking for weakness anywhere in the body

feeling the strength in marcus arms and legs
making his stomach and back work
satisfied no apparent weakness was there
we broke off and circled each other
he ran and jumped at me trying for a splash
but i easily sidestepped
spun a glancing side kick to his head
facing me
he tried a reverse back kick
spinning in a half circle
my defense dropping to one knee
then pivoting with my leg extended
sweeping his legs out from under him
with an elbow drop I dove on him
he double chopped me on my neck
receiving a knee back to his face
then marcus caught me in a bear hug
but i twisted out using my legs as levers
then a bell clap to his ears
to release me
up and facing each other again
his next move
a head butt to my body
got him a knee strike to his face
then i wielded a two handed double axe handle
with a blow to the side of his head
knocking him over
slamming him hard and pinning his shoulders
down for the count and he lost
sweat poured off us
as we bowed to augustus
come at noon tomorrow and bring lazarus
he commanded as he stepped out
thanking marcus i departed

*

at the villa of augustus the next day
there he introduced us to his son and heir tiberius
after eating and watching some dancers
augustus began to spool out a yarn
he said years ago he had sailed east to syria

going there to convince tiberius to return to rome
tiberius had been in self imposed exile for years
the heir must learn the ways of rome he said
tiberius had taken him to a temple by the sea of galilee
a temple to the patron of virgins the goddess diana
twin sister to the god apollo famous at delphi
at a ceremony of the full moon at dianas temple
tiberius urged me to spread my seed into a virgin
yes i told him to create real sons tiberius said
even bastard sons at least have some of your blood
better than an adopted son like me to be his heir
the mantle of a son must be earned augustus said
whether adopted or not a princeps must have merit
there in the temple steeped in wine was a virgin mary
your mother mary tiberius confirmed
my mother was never at a pagan temple in judea
yes she was given the fruit of the vine to honor diana
augustus placed his seed in her tiberius claimed
from his seed you are his own son
look at yourself in this mirror jesus
compare yourself to that wall fresco
you have the same look he had when he was your age
you have his turquoise blue eyes his fair skin
his blond hair turned dark as witnesses
behold augustus follows augustus
augustus did you tell mary that you were an angel
my mother told me i was born to her from an angel
that is her fantasy augustus said
she could not speak my language so i told her nothing
tiberius stated that he had paid her father to use her
then gave her back with a dowry for a husband
many servants have been paid to watch over you jesus
as you grew as a secret son of augustus
you are julius caesars adopted son i said to augustus
why aren't you content with your adopted son tiberius
he does not want to be princeps augustus answered
he resists taking on the responsibilities
that is true tiberius said it does not appeal to me
the army of rome offers more to its commanders
than the senate does to its princeps

you could put the senators on the army payroll
and they would still mutiny
how do i fit into all of this lazarus asked
you are my son tiberius answered
your mother was my virgin at the temple
you are both our sons
but before you are accepted as true sons
you must prove that you have roman iron in your veins
you must conquer some lands for rome
we are sending you on a voyage augustus decreed
a test like jason and the golden fleece
or like the tasks of heracles tiberius added
you are to take a ship loaded with iron goods
sail to africa and trade these goods for gold
how is trading conquering for rome lazarus asked
rome is built on commerce tiberius replied
wars are just trade disputes my son
augustus as an adopted son of julius proved worthy
my task is to follow in augustus footsteps as a worthy son
but if i fail we need reserve troops
bastard sons must prove themselves worthy
this is the first step on your paths
following us in the glory of rome
jah will prove to be what he proves to be i said
augustus please look in my eyes to see my god jah
read the visions in my eyes as my eyes kiss yours
in your eyes augustus I see a line of great rulers
men and women stepping forward from history
each forbearer a noble ruler senators and generals
beautiful graceful and elegant women
each one greeting me as my eyes move into your depths
there is a line of great rulers in your eyes too
i see myself in your eyes jesus
your eyes look for julius as your father
my eyes are the way in to my father jah
my god whose adopted son i wish to be
this eye embrace senses visionary insights
my eyes are more sky blue yours are oceans
we are like sorcerers divining signs
augustus said as he sipped his wine

you are no priest jesus
this is the proposition
we are lending you one hundred talents
in iron trade goods
go with your friend lazarus
leave rome
take ship with traders we have arranged for
bring the glory of roman iron in trade for gold
my weight in gold back to me
sail past carthage
sail thru the gates to the ends of the earth
south along the coast of africa
south to a great forest
rivers where black people rule
trade with them
live with them
this voyage will prove to us
your fathers augustus and tiberius
what sort of men jesus and lazarus are
when you know your true gods
the gods of your fathers
return to me in rome in two years time
pay back my weight in gold
caesar may find you worthy of honor
men to walk in our footsteps
the princeps commands
go now

*

tiberius followed us out and told us
you know that sixteen bronze ass coins
are traded for one silver denarius
twenty five silver denarius trade for one gold aureus
augustus weight is twelve thousand aureus
that is only enough to pay an army of thirty thousand
for a month when each man costs ten denarius a month
it is a challenge for good men to prove themselves
tiberius took us to the soldiers barracks
he introduced us to the ship captain bonoba
bonoba was a black man from the far african coast
he was a roman citizen and centurion

the men in his crew were all romans loyal to tiberius
they had served him in his eastern campaigns
all the crew were mixed tribes from many lands
men from all over some blond others red headed
most with hair brown or black
the one very dark hair and skin was commander bonoba
*

V

the ship with forty men set sail two days later
sometimes rowed sometimes wind sailed
first to carthage then west along the coast
our iron axes our iron hoes and tools
heavy in the hull kept for trade
it will take ten thousand denarius just to pay these men
two years is a long voyage and they are seasoned
sailors better than any since jason the captain said
we sailed months stopping only for water and food
at ports bonoba knew along the way
he taught me sailing skills
more skill for the wide ocean
how to take advantage of the wind
a month along the coast
a harsh desert along the shore without ports
lazarus was content knowing of tiberius
as his true father saying he knew it was true
augustus is not my father
unless my mother confesses it to be true
my father has always been joseph not an angel
mother was just calling him that out of love
but jesus you do not look like your brothers and sisters
that does not make me a son of augustus
he is father to everyone who is a roman
we disputed these ideas for many days
tiberius and augustus gave us seed thoughts from satan
selfish ideas to grow in our minds
romans believe all gods are equal
worship any god you like
worship through idols if you like
curse gods who don't help you
they embrace satans struggle to be at the top
there is no such thing as a day of rest
cast your parents aside and become yourself
satan says murder anyone who gets in your way

these romans want us to become like them
take whatever we want or desire
take from those who have more than you
lie if you have to just like satan
advice from the master liar
jealousy is natural
take from people richer than you
cheat them for a fortune
get more for yourself
you are the most important person in the world
these are the seeds of satan
we must cast these out of our minds lazarus
jesus he said you doubt yourself
tiberius and augustus are only men
tiberius is likely my father
doubting old augustus is understandable
but he is not full of satan

*

finally we came to the green jungle
only captain bonoba had been there before
the mouth of the two rivers into a coastal lagoon
entered by a narrow channel to a village there
friendly people the asante people
the captain spoke their language
our men built a fort there as a base
further along the coast were the guan
followers of the warrior king named ghana
three days march along the coast led to their territory
a river named pra was there rich in gold
the people called the kong lived upriver
below the kong mountains
gold was in the river gravels
we built sluices and used iron shovels to feed gravel
water ran over ripples in the troughs to get gold out
the asante people learned to work the sluices
they loved the iron tools as wages

*

the trade was iron for gold
ten iron for one weight gold
at this rate it would take four years to gather gold

enough to just satisfy payment to caesar
we decided to reach out to the guan people
they agreed to build and work sluices too
they went up river for more plentiful metal
lazarus and i went up river with them
the guan teaching lazarus about medicine plants
healing plants poison plants
my questions were who are your gods
how do you worship them
they told me stories made of iron endurance
traded for my stories of gold about jah
in the villages they heard my stories
the asante and the guan accepted the love of jah
people learned the eye embrace
the wisdom teaching of colors
the people built a temple
as jah designed through me
a temple of song
round and wide with a round balcony inside
the people began to sing in the temple
the men in deep voices each adding to the next
the women in sweet voices in the wind
bouncing off each other floating in the air
the children all around the balcony
holding back until the end of a song

*

the songs started slowly
the men and a deep heartbeat
echoing in mountains of rumbling thunder
the songs with women in groups with harmony
building to a crescendo like love making back and forth
topped with the piercing clear bells of children
notes of song birds sweet honey
there i was in the centre of the circle
calling on each and blending the voices
join a song they sang
sing dusty and deep
dance dusty and deep
touch dusty and deep

round earth round time
brown earth brown bodies
we dance in the eye of jah
round bodies of deep time
round bodies of deep space
floating in the green sea
swimming in the old time
round dust in the gold time
round earth dancing round bodies
to sing in the old time
to touch deep dust
jah dance jah sing jah touch
sing dusty and deep
sing the black touch
sing the white touch
dance red bodies dance blue sea
spin red dust spin gold dust
sing in the old time
see gold dust in the old time
we dance we sing we touch
floating in the red and white
swimming in the blue time
round earth round bodies
sing jah dusty and deep
dance jah dusty and deep
touch jah dusty and deep
sing high sweet jah
touch life mighty jah
swim in the green sea
fly in the heaven
see the way in
fly to jah sing to jah
hold jah touch jah
dance round jah
see the way in
fly to jah sing to jah
hold jah touch jah
sing together dance together
touch together see together

*

some of the sailors joined in the songs
yet they clung to their weapons
peoples from the surrounding areas came to see us
women warriors in a group called hausa
dressed for battle with spears and bows came
over one hundred women strong
these women admired the weapons of my men
they suggested they would trade protection for us for a year
if they were then given some knives and swords and shields
captain bonoba agreed that on our departure
they would be rewarded for their services

*

some people known as the kong
came to my camp with their prince desmong
who ruled them from the land of mali
beyond the place that captain bonoba came from
the prince offered me a bag of clear stones
triangle shaped stones in trade for iron hoes
stones that sparkled in the sun and were harder than steel
they cut anything
make good arrow tips he said
they would be good jewelry for roman ladies bonoba said
after i agreed he invited the captain and me to visit his palace
he took us up trails as i learned his language better
bonoba was more of a kong man
through passes in the kong mountains
we came to his village where people rejoiced to see him
many days later on a high plateau
the princes mud brick palace stood
it was surrounded by some date palm trees
grasslands and scattered garden plots
hundreds of small houses in all directions
his family had great herds of goats
the measure of their wealth
producing much milk and cheese
many people came to him and bowed down in worship
people offered him children to sacrifice
he selected twins a boy and a girl

lambs about six years old
these he had dressed in luxurious gowns
they were paraded through the palace
at dawn the next morning they were to be sacrificed
offered to the flying god bird of the sky
a giant statue was in a temple
they called this angel bird jah
the sacrifice was a command started by jah
when he ordered the king to sacrifice his son
desmong confessed that he had never seen the sky god
the god named jah had never been seen by anyone
jah is my god i told him
then i told the true story of abraham
how jah stayed his hand from killing issac
desmong listened to me preach to stop child sacrifice
my god the only god no longer wants this
as gods messenger i have come
to teach your people a new way
the angel of jah hears me
if you do not listen to me I will call on him
to visit you in your sleep
carry you alive and screaming over a volcano
bubbling red hot earth and brimstone
jah will drop you in and you will burn forever
i do not believe you jesus he said
you must wrestle me
and the winner will get his way
so i wrestled with desmong in the dark
he had great power but i danced away into shadows
stopped still and listened the dolphin way
when he came i swept his feet away
and held him in a choke hold
until he gave in
you have no need for jah he said
when you can wrestle like that
*

a great crowd arrived before dawn
desmong stood at the high altar
he drew a gold dagger

two young goats were presented for slaughter
he spoke out to the people in their language
all of you were children once
all of you have value to the highest god
you must sacrifice only what is good to eat
children are not to be sacrificed
no people young or old are to be killed
our god is a god of love i added
today is a new way to worship a new god
my teaching is today you must begin construction
build a round temple dedicated to jah
learn to sing praises to jah
prince desmong has the blessing of jah
child sacrifice is no more for his people
captives and slaves are not to be sacrificed
there is a new way to let god in
all the people must listen to my teaching
after you accept the new way and exchanges of eyes
tear down the idol to jah
an omen will occur
millions of butterflies will come down from the sky
all the colors of rainbows
blessings from jah
then it came to pass that the annual descent of butterflies
was an omen to the blessings of jah
rather than acceptance of child sacrifice
as it had been before
with that it was goodbye to the people of mali
the lesson that i learned
preaching fire and brimstone threats does not work

*

while i was away lazarus had gone south in a boat
with a guide to see the tribe of little people called efe
little people half the height of other people
to learn their medicine both good and bad
blow tubes with poison darts to kill birds and monkeys
weeds gathered for brew to bring joy and music
three of these efe people had come to the camp
the two left behind offered to take me there

the leader of the two named sua said that it was far away
it would take about three moons to get there
a moon along the ocean shore to the mouth of the river
another moon to get around the rapids and waterfalls
inland to where the river was smooth
another moon of paddling up the mighty river
then on trails through the jungle
captain bonoba had the gold coming in steady
another year would bring in profits
there was peace around us with woman warriors
the two efe people passed around some pipes
to smoke a weed they carried the happy weed
much like the wine of greece with dancing
every day was a celebration when smoking it
so i journeyed with them in search of lazarus
after fifteen days we passed a large estuary
another great river called niger flooded out to us
the people there shot arrows at us so i dug into the paddles
sua claimed yoruba people hate efe people
we kill them quick and they are too slow to catch us
not the time to test his idea paddle harder
finally we got to the mightiest river flowing into the sea
not as great as the nile but still magnificent
the trek was along the banks
climbing higher and higher
the canyon was full of rapids beside us as we hiked up
we came to a huge lake
an estuary of the river
backed up from a natural dam of hard rock
there a village on the lake with big friendly people
they spoke a kong tongue
called the river kongo
the efe traded an iron knife of mine
for another boat and we paddled upstream
along the river we saw many animals
as sua taught me his very musical language
he told me that he and his friends had been on a quest
searching the world for any small people like them
sometimes big people have children who grow up small

individuals in parts of the world i have seen
they had not formed tribes though like yours
we finally reached a waterfall called boyoma
up trails we encountered animals that were almost people
very hairy efe people sua suggested
he called the place of the animals bonobo
the same name as my captain i asked
different bonobo not bonoba sua said
these animals are the bono of bonobo near boyoma
too many bees buzzing here i said
better the bonos use body language to talk
they look more like men than monkeys
they chewed the weeds the same as the efe smoked
the bonos laughed and played with us
followed us on the trail for a while
soon we came to the first efe village
lazarus was there a giant in their midst
you think you are a god here lazarus
not all giants are gods he laughed
we had hoes and shovels and broad swords
between us much iron to work with
the gardens grew plantains nuts beans palm kernels
many greens and herbs to eat a new diet
lazarus knew their language and introduced me
first to the chiefs then many others
especially a beautiful young woman
he was bewitched by umbee
a woman shaman
in her hut umbee made the magic medicines
her eyes opened to me in the ritual way
deep dark eyes of earth embraced me
the visionary insights of her eyes
there were bonos bouncing in her eyes
a row of animals bearing gifts to me
gifts for teaching lazarus
the secrets of the forest
she passed his love back
with kisses to my hands
a great show from all her people

songs and dances all day all night
much like my temple creation back at camp
these people already had the music of creation
a few days later lazarus came to me
lets go with her to see the old forest mother
umbee took us through the forest
she followed some large footprints in the mud
feet that made marks like hands four handed people
we met them the size of bears but much gentler
playful like the bonos
grinners lazarus called them great grinners
we sat in a circle and umbee passed some herbs to them
we chewed together
a warm glow came over us
a contentment that led to sleep
under the giant leaves
a big silverback papa snored beside me
umbee crawled over to a very old woman grinner
they held each other rocking forehead to forehead
mind to mind i heard them talking
umbee asked about marrying lazarus
having big children would kill you the grinner said
small efe women must marry only efe men

*

after a moon passed at the village i told lazarus
it is time to go back to our own camp
no he resisted i will stay here with umbee
i am in love with her and want to marry her
no umbee said go with jesus
she fed him some powder and brew
after he vomited his eyes were opened wide
he could see the way was best with me
with tears in his eyes he kissed her and accepted it
she told us she would come with us for a little ways
there was a young bono we need to meet
then we left the efe people and took the jungle trail
a few days later we were surrounded by bonos
umbee touched foreheads with the old grandmother leader
it was decided that ten year old female nana

56

an adopted daughter of umbee
was to go with lazarus to keep him company
a daughter of hers to share with him
in bono ways it is the boys who stay
it is the females
who are sent away
*

nana was full of fun and tricks
we laughed all the way back to camp
from the first day we saw something else as well
when she was afraid or happy or for no reason
she liked to rub her pleasure spot
between her legs
soothing the same as holding hands or hugging
rubbing herself on lazarus like he was her family
expressing delight as she heated up
sometimes bothersome and in the way of doing anything
like a dog that always wants petting
nana was sensitive and wanted to be accepted
when lazarus scolded her for rubbing on others
she kept it to herself
in the night alone she rubbed herself
by the time we got to our camp
nana and her way was more like people than bono
*

the men who had stayed at the river mouth
like odysseus men not covering their ears
all had fallen for the black siren women
gold was worthless compared to love
the warrior women had ministered a potion
a potion from the roots of a love bush
given to the men it left them enthralled
it aroused them and made them bond
loyal to their bones to the women
they had married these beauties to stay
some of the hausa women already had thick bellies
only ten soldiers could be persuaded to sail back
so long as their wives could come too
all the iron not traded was left

for the men who stayed behind
captain bonoba led the group going back
it was really the wives that sailed bringing their men
they brought amphorae of potion to last a long time
the control of the men was the magic in the drinks
nana just loved all the touching and caressing
trying to include herself everywhere
*

along the coast i called to the dolphins
to share our company leaping beside the boat
this they did from time to time
dolphins like to play first
a heavy boat is not much fun
we were not in a hurry and the men were in love
the fresh fish dolphins corralled to our net
fish were energy for our own rowing
energy for the lovemaking of the newly wed too
one of the dolphins ringee
took an interest in nana
who was soon swimming with dolphins
she took to the water easily
clung to ringee soon riding
like lazarus and me
my wish my creative will for fair winds
found favor with jah
two years later at the age eighteen
rome took us in again
*

after setting aside the weight of gold
owed to augustus we divided the rest equally
twelve shares of five thousand aureus each
fortunes enough to pay an army of one thousand for a year
yet the gold did not bring me joy
lazarus continued to wish he had stayed with the efe people
but we went to the stables and saw the stallions
golden eye and lucifer cheered us
nana proceeded to pet and hug them
*

augustus had died some time before

we paid the gold owed to his heir
the new princeps tiberius
was delighted that lazarus was successful
berius hosted a celebration in our honor
the men with black wives paraded to the senators wives
as women who knew how to please their men
yet it was the men who pleased their women
roman wives fancied themselves as masters too
these women were like goddesses in their eyes
tiberius asked lazarus to leave nana at the lodgings with a slave
no telling what the roman women would think of her behavior
at the games roman women ignored the gladiators
fascinated by the black goddesses
tiberius and the men watched the gladiators
we saw an egyptian battling a german giant
that reminded me of david and goliath
entertainment on a grand scale
other cohorts of slaves slew lions from africa
chariot races were cheered by the crowds
with tiberius again winning the main event
he proudly wore his own winning laurels
from the ninety fourth olympiad
we sat and watched him driving his chariot
behind our horses golden eye and lucifer
whipping them with lashes they ran with fear
winning he laughed at their battle scars
afterwards at his stables he bragged
with such brave horses enemies will cower
see what great caesar tiberius has done
he has turned your horses into horse demigods
all for the glory of rome

*

at his villa in the same manner as augustus
tiberius was a new man happy to be princeps
he told us he was the true son
he had proven himself as a general for augustus
then as a master of the revels of rome
he spoke as a musician played a pipe
to lure a snake to rise in a basket

he repeated the story of augustus
he himself took the princeps to a secret temple to bed virgins
augustus had a legitimate but barren wife
my mother livia tiberius said
barren after my brother drusus and i were born
no man could get child from her
augustus was my step father but he wanted his own sons
livia allowed augustus to do this
she even recruited me to help him
he promised that any sons born like you jesus
would not come to rome
on this note like an actors cue livia appeared
yes jesus i convinced augustus to let his bastards
grow in the wilderness
the better to be free of the intrigue of rome she said
now i am a widow but still rule as an empress
yes you do resemble augustus i see she said
but there is no place for you here jesus
my son has replaced the line of augustus
banishment is too good for jesus he should be crucified
no mother there is noble blood on both sides of our histories
any and all sons must prove their worth tiberius insisted
he could be useful in the eastern provinces
you lazarus are my best bastard son
one of a batch of bastards now grown up
that whore daughter of augustus that I was married to
gave me no legitimate children
yet he would not let me divorce her
do not be too harsh livia said his divorce laws kept me in power
augustus had sent men to watch over you jesus
he had paid favors to educate and cultivate you
but you are a weed too pampered livia stated
king herod was supposed to root you out
yet like a grapevine grown in the wilderness
far from the garden of rome you have flourished
but now we must clear the fields
tiberius says you may live if you return to judea
return to your jewish family
take root as a lemon tree there

you are not welcome here jesus
there is no place and no role for an actor like you
you are no soldier and we have enough teachers
yet you could make him a gladiator tiberius
it would give me pleasure to watch him die that way
no mother jesus is banished from rome and sentenced to judea
but i am a generous and kind ruler
if judea does not suit you jesus
you are allowed one other direction
you may travel east
travel as a trader or a teacher
under pain of death never mention augustus again
become someone little or someone great on your own merits
be a forgotten priest of your god jah if you wish
while i live never lay eyes on rome again
as for you my son lazarus you must serve me
in the riots of entertainment for the mob
augustus taught me that it is not war that gives power
it is showmanship and spectacle that gives power
you will serve me and rise up in the ranks
*

at dawn to our lodgings lazarus came with a warning
the mother of tiberius is mad
livia has murder in mind
after you left she continued to say that you are a threat
she wants your life is to be taken
you must go quickly jesus
after she left tiberius got drunk with me
angry with his mother for telling him what to do
he hates women who take charge over men
blamed the black wives of our sailors as examples
for showing roman women how to be in charge
over my objections he said he would show rome
what happens to such women
he ordered his men to kill five of the black wives
five of our sailors too if they got in the way
in his drunken rage tiberius wants all the gold
he does not like the example of husbands as slaves
he wants the black warrior women wiped out

if we stay assassins will come for us all
warnings have been sent to the men
meet us at the docks at our boat
in a moment i had packed and was leaving
lazarus had horses tied below
golden eye and lucifer held by nana
the barn master thinks i am just exercising them
she can ride or double behind me
our ship awaits and these horses will soon be missed
we found saddle bags for our gold
we packed it in and lazarus instructed the servant
take back this note to caesars villa
along with this bag of gold as compensation
gold in exchange for the horses
the horses pounded
all the way to the distant dock
the news was five men and five women were dead
captain bonoba and four other men and their wives
were at the ship ready to sail
we loaded the horses and cast off

*

we sailed quickly to judea ahead of any pursuers
there we found a roman lawyer
lazarus had taken horses illegally
compensation had been paid
the lawyer took us to the roman governor
the sailors paid another fine in gold as compensation
for their discharge from the navy
the governor would write to the senate
telling them that he had heard the issue
decreed the matter was settled
taking fine gold
he discharged us each to go our own way
the men with their wives back to africa
except for bonoba and his wife who went to alexandria
along with lazarus and nana
who rode the horse lucifer
only i stayed in galilee
along with golden eyes

VI

on to nazareth to see my family
there my mother was a widow
the family head was now james
joseph had died of fever the year before
after visiting his grave i had a family meeting
all my brothers and sisters loved james
yet here was a guest a distant brother
a stranger in their home a visitor
james would stay as head i would be the feet
there was some gold to buy some property
some gold to provide food for the needy
a poor family my needy family
we had a feast and celebrated
alone at last with my mother mary
she would answer no questions directly
your conception and birth were from angels
the evidence is the way that all animals love you she said
they want jesus as their wise master
you are just like those wise men from the east
they warned me to take you to egypt
jah saved you from king herod
joseph knew herod wanted you dead
augustus wife livia was behind it
joseph saved you too and he believed me
that you were from an angel
you really believe this mother
yes i do
my prayers to gabriel were answered
jah put his seed in me
jah is my father
let me look into your eyes mother
there are two colors in your irises
around the centre black hole there is a dark brown circle
chestnuts

these are surrounded with a cool ocean blue
the chestnuts have secrets inside them
it was not comfortable for me
to look deeper
to try to crack open the shells
my sight broke away from the visionary insights
*

during my year in nazareth i spent some time
making myself some golden rings
one hundred and forty four rings
the gold was for longevity not for value
each ring was inscribed with the star constellation
the wain the wagon of heaven pointing north
the shape of a chariot carved on each ring
the north star on each a white triangle from my bag
jewels that prince desmong had traded me
each triangle worked into a six pointed star of david
these triangle gems were known as diamonds
also a dolphin symbol signaling swimming
travelling on a journey
my travels were to be journeys of friendship
each ring was made to go to a true set of eyes
six to my close family mother brothers and sisters
other rings were for friends met along the way
to take on my journey into the unknown
tying each ring to the next with a bit of yarn
string links sewed into my sash
worn around the waist as a travellers belt
each new friend to give a ring to
each ring to seal a friendship
*

the word is a wind
words in action are a force blowing
sometimes words come from jah in the wind
singing in the wind on a galloping horse
after a year the wind stirred me to travel
to ride to alexandria
to visit with lazarus nana and old david
lazarus had written letters to me
he said he would continue to live in alexandria

he had a letter from tiberius forgiving him
begging him to return to rome
lazarus said no i am learning to be a doctor
healing the sick and wounded here
applying my learning to help those in need
my special medicines like milk of poppy for pain
black bellflower berries for body sleep
a sharp knife to slice out sick growths
the hashish from arabia to sharpen appetite
leaves and preparations for potions
medicine for all manner of ills
an amphora of the love potion too
even some poison from the efe for dart tips
if tiberius sends agents after me
blow darts for them

*

returning to alexandria
honey colored alexandria
directly at the library i met david first
he took me to see
lazarus and nana at the sick peoples section of the city
lazarus was working with the doctors there
nana was a nurse for his charges
with warm rejoicing we hugged
enjoyed our eyes sensing visionary insights
davids eyes were olive trees filled with doves
soft grey with tans and silver blues
nanas eyes were lonely eggs on a cliff face
afraid of falling into a stormy sea
lazarus told me that he was going to return to galilee
his calling was to help his family and the jewish people
he did not feel like a roman
we decided to get provisions for a celebration at the market
the first person we met was captain bonoba
he was a trader at the market
he had changed his name to philip
to avoid notice which was impossible
with his dark warrior wife noruba
philip insisted we celebrate with wine
music and dance on the streets

later that night noruba got into a fight
drew her sword and killed an egyptian
which caused a general melee
friends of the egyptian took revenge
noruba was killed and philip deeply wounded
hundreds of rats came to our defense
drove the fighters away
how did this happen i wondered
david told me that he now spoke with rats through his mind
you see jesus the minds of the rats
surrendered to me
when i prayed to jehovah to help me
the seeds of satan can be plucked out of minds
of animals as well as people
the book that i am writing at the library
contains all the secrets of how to do this
so what does my friend nana say in her mind
david stared at her
she wants to hump me
no she says just hug
your prayers are answered lazarus laughed
prayers help open minds my boy
so open your tongue david
share your secrets
like who paid you to tutor me
yes he admitted some romans from augustus
had offered me coin to teach you
but i took none
it was my honor to be witness
to your quick learning
*

lazarus used his medicines to mend philip
we stayed in his tent and nursed him
when he was back on his feet
he received a friendship ring
along with a promise to see him again
the love potion from noruba had worn off
he knew that she was destined for her violent end
those who live by the sword
meet death by the sword

*

david had not shared his rat mind talking with anyone
saving his conclusions for the codex he was writing
he shared all he knew with me
the rats were very good at solving puzzles and mazes
they helped each other yet were always striving to dominate
the words in their minds were simple
there was little beyond the moment
sneak sniff chew bite where is the food
what does the leader want
other than the marvel of being able to listen
and project commands to them
it is not very inspiring i said
well they do not sing and dance david admitted
but they do make useful slaves
they came to our defense in the fight
i have a present for you jesus
here is a prince of rats to accompany you
his name is sam after samuel
hello sam i said to his mind
through his eyes as i looked into him
it was not a dialogue like talking
more a door to read inside him
lazarus had his friend nana as a gift
now i had a gift friend too

*

why are you on a quest david asked me
there is much wisdom to learn in the world
knowledge and understanding are what i seek
everything you need to know is here in the library
some words in the library are just nuts off a tree
the tree itself needs to be seen in its full glory
there are stories and thoughts of great teachers in the east
masters of people like buddha right here in the library
by going to the source of the rivers of knowledge
the waters will be purer
nuts are not the whole tree and all water starts with rain
then you must see for yourself jesus
with our eyes embracing he accepted a golden ring
finally i asked please send me with a letter

to a friend of yours
whoever dwells the farthest east
david gave me the letter that i asked for
sent me to meet saul and his wife rachael
across to a port on the red sea
lazarus and nana came along
on their way to galilee
we rode the horses there
when we departed each other at the red sea
he agreed to take the horses back with him
the great heart of golden eye said farewell
nana winked as she hugged lucifer
sam was asleep in my bag

*

a week was spent with saul and his wife rachael
we traded stories and songs and teachings
eye embraces of color and pictures
each received a golden ring of friendship
a heart to heart hug from both and their children
my new friend saul took me to mount sinai
where he camped at the base while i went on alone
in an ascent to the summit to meet jah
a fire at the end of the day to keep warm
alone on the summit of mount sinai
only sam to pet and feed
for two days nothing happened
hearing only a voice in my mind speaking
these are simple commandments
written on your heart jesus
THE WAY IN IS LOVE
LOVE AND HONOR THE CREATOR
WITH YOUR WHOLE BEING
LOVE AND HONOR OTHERS AS YOURSELF
a dream came on the second night
a great bird creature rose up from behind trees
beautiful long feathers a huge man like bird
it flew circling and calling in hebrew
LITTLE JESUS
YOU HAVE BEEN WATCHED BY JAH
SINCE YOU WERE BORN

SOME OF US SPEAK IN A VOICE THAT IS THE WAY IN
LISTEN INSIDE YOURSELF TO MY WORDS
MY NAME IS GABRIEL
LISTEN TO ME
YOU WILL SEE ME AS AN ANGEL IN THE MATERIAL WORLD
AS A GIANT BIRD FROM HEAVEN
AS A VOICE OF JAH
OTHERS HEAR OTHER ANGELS
SOME LISTEN TO SATAN THE RESISTOR ANGEL
WHO CLAIMS JEHOVAH IS DEAD
WE LIVE HUNDREDS OF YEARS EVEN A THOUSAND YEARS
THERE ARE FEW OF US LEFT ON THIS EARTH
HUMANS WHO REFUSE OUR WORDS IN THEIR MINDS
ARE REFUSING THE GREAT CREATOR
WE OF THE LONG TIME MIND
WORSHIP IN OUR MINDS
SHARING OUR WORDS
YOU HEAR ME JESUS BECAUSE YOU ARE BLESSED
ONLY A FEW PEOPLE CAN HEAR US
MOST RESIST AS IS THEIR NATURE
SATANS FOLLOWERS ARE ALSO RESISTORS
AS IS THEIR NATURE
gabriels foot claw pointed to a rock tablet
the two new commandments etched on it
then all was quiet sleep
silence
in the morning i awoke
there was no tablet
when i returned to camp
saul had written a letter to a friend
for me to carry to his loved one
who dwelt the farthest east
this was to be the pattern
the way in friendship
from sinai saul took a path to the sea
there were two boats there at the dock
one for saul to return to his rachael
the other boat leaving with six pearl divers
seven including me

*

we would find pearls along the way
trading these at a port called jedda
there to find sauls friend lucinius
a wine merchant and innkeeper
along the way the pearl divers
showed how to retrieve the shellfish
open these to find a pearl
the meat from the shellfish was delicious
sweet fragrant chewy and full
the old laws for food are for tasteless people
no poison in this shellfish
this meat is never from a sacrifice to false gods
yes the meat from pigs can give you worms
if there is a reason not to eat then abstain
anything can be eaten if you use common sense
as sam groaned with a full belly
lots of good meat
but pearls were few
my call went out to dolphins
who came and aided in finding the beds of shellfish
they ate the insides after we searched for pearls
these dolphins quickly learned how to become
deep divers for bigger shellfish
soon pearls were located
as each man was given oysters
each pouch began to have a few pearls
my dolphin friend found one that was very large
as a delight for me to trade at jedda
*

lucinius took the letter from saul
asked many questions of mount sinai
the new commandments and jah
we spoke late into the night
lucinius shared some wine and hashish to eat
hashish was a medicine lazarus had
this is very strong hashish lucinius said
giving a small piece to sam
soon we were laughing about everything
rolling on his carpet
we are on a visionary carpet ride he chuckled

but i hear my mistress calling me for another kind of ride
so i must leave you until the morning
he left me thinking my ride was to sleep there
as i lay on the carpet it began to move
visions flying on it came to me in my imagination
the confinement of the room and my senses full
the walls burst and fell away
a vast expanse of space opened up around me
in rapture i was wrapped in light
all the colors of the world whirled about me
emotions whirled inside me like wings of a bird
suddenly i was alongside of gabriel
over mount sinai
next my carpet flew over the great pyramids
they glowed with golden limestone
at its pinnacle my carpet alighted
looking down the sides at the blocks of the pyramid
they seemed formed by blocks of hashish
this made me laugh and sailing off over the desert
my carpet seemed made out of pearls and precious gems
flashing many crystal colors amethyst purple
red rubies yellow amber and topaz and diamonds
blue sapphires and green emeralds all living and pulsing
delicious perfumes filled the air
essences of flowers fruits spices delighted my nose
cinnamon cloves cardamom apricot and nutmeg
next the carpet spun into blackness
when the room came back i was still laughing
still in the house of lucinius
filled with divine energy alive in triumph

*

a few days later lucinius loaded up some camels
rode with me to mecca
to the real temple of jah
that abraham built
to a place that lucinius had described to me
at mecca the tabernacle of abraham
contained three hundred and sixty five dolls
one doll as an idol to worship each day
to honor stories of gods and heroes

a library like alexandria with each idol
handled by a priest to remember a story
a few were goddess dolls held by priestesses
laughing i asked them
do pilgrims come on carpets
to listen to you priestesses lie about gods and goddesses
jah has abandoned this place i see
they pointed to the black stone in the corner
it came like a star from heaven to earth
where did earth come from is the question
all things are made first in heaven
this whole world is a rock spinning in heaven
my world is on this spinning carpet
then i confronted the priests and priestesses
there is no truth in your stories of these idols
it is better for this place to lay desolate
than to be occupied by false worship
they gathered together against me
drew knives
you get out of here
you and your dirty little rat
*

let me tell you a prophecy i have for you
you have rejected me and my god jehovah
the true god of this place
at a future time
another prophet will come to this place
the angel gabriel will lead him here
he will throw out your idols by force of arms
this temple will be reestablished
the centre of the world of a new prophet
you have rejected me who comes in peace
all that i have is laughter at your dolls
the new prophet will destroy you and all your descendants
he will have visions stories and songs from god
told to him by the angel gabriel
you reject me as one man but he will have many followers
to bring destruction to priests of idols
to smote you with death not laughter
you have rejected my way to the creator

my way of peace and love will be replaced by the next prophet
for his followers he will teach songs
that welcome strangers with hospitality
that command protection for guests
but death to idolaters like you
no hospitality to you
he will allow a path for his followers
to hear the miracle of my song
when my words are finally revealed
all my love glowing in a mist of time
my way in will be revealed at a later time
all who seek god will find me then

*

the idolater priests chased me away
closing ears for hundreds of years
until the prophesy is fulfilled

*

that night in jedda i told lucinius to remember my words
my prophesy here for future generations
and to pass down the parable of old aesop
a parable for followers of a future prophet
a young master had a horse and a dog
the dog would play toss stick
stand on its hind legs
roll over
jump on the lap to be petted
the master fed him choice table scraps
the horse would run fast to please the master
walk slow and jump over logs on command
for his reward of straw grass
but the horse became jealous of the dog
so one day he played toss the bit
he stood on his hind legs
and then rolled over and lay on the master
the master was outraged and hit the horse with a stick
never rode him again just hitched him to a plow
in my parable the master is jah
the new prophet is the horse and jesus is the dog
horses will never be lap dogs
followers must be content with who they are

the favor of jah provides music for each kind
when this song of jesus is heard
those who first heard the next prophets songs
loved his words thundering on the road
those will love jesus words in their laps
the music of prophets are miracles
the poetry of the prophets are pearls
nacre nourishes the nugget
remember me as the rabbi born to reign
as the prince of peace on jahs lap
when the wind of jah stirs the world again
*

back in jedda at the market
a man had heard about the special pearl
all that i have is yours for this pearl
would you trade everything for this pearl
yes everything that i have
even your wife and children and your soul
everything even my soul
the love of this pearl has consumed your life
it shames me to hold it
here take it as a gift
what can i give you in return
you have nothing of value
everything you had is already taken in desire
your love for a thing has left you with nothing
even your soul is worth nothing
*

the way in is better than a great pearl
that a merchant would sell all he has to own
the way in is a milky pearl in the milky way
a star gazer sees in the north star
a great pearl to follow home
*

lucinius learned the way in of the eyes
insights of color and smell
we shared an embrace of eyes ritual
lucinius clasped his golden ring
a ring to give away all he had he said
and follow the way with me

not for the ring for the friendship
it is not yet the time for followers
just a letter to a friend towards the east
a small boat he gave me took me onward
to his sister in law in yemen
a widow sheba her namesake the queen
who had married king solomon

*

VII

sheba lived a very rich life in a large villa
with many servants all from her late husband
the brother of lucinius named sibilius who had died
a year previous in a fight with pirates
sheba dressed in silk and used delicate perfumes
wearing her rich dark hair curled in roman fashion
sheba loved old stories tales of cleopatra
she begged news of alexandria of greece of rome
especially words of lucinius her brother in law
she welcomed the little prince sam like her own child

*

our eyes kissed as soon as they met
the color of her eyes was dark gold honey
shebas table held sweet pears apricots nuts
savory spices in the meats intoxicated the breath
music from lyres played by talented slaves
red wine smelling of rich earth berries licorice

*

from the book of the song of solomon
sheba sang
the song of sheba shimmers on the sea
my eyes are those of doves my love
rest on beds of boughs in a house of cedar
the smell of junipers awakens us
as saffron comes in from the coastal plain
there is a lily among thorny weeds
a beauty amid the plain girls
an apple tree standing alone in the forest
shade for you in the hot sun
there to sit and be refreshed
with apples with cakes of raisins with wine
let my left hand cup your head
let my right hand embrace you
the gazelles leaping by us
the hinds of the forest dancing by us

awaken love if it suits you my love
the voice of the turtledove is in the tree above
blossoms are in the land sweet perfume
the time of vine trimming has arrived
on my bed during the nights
i have sought one whom my soul has loved
but i did not find him
i rose up and went around the city
in the streets and in the squares i sought him
but i did not find him
hear my voice bring pleasure
look at my beautiful form my dear one
he is gone among the lilies
until the day breathes and the shadows flee
he is gone with the gazelles
gone with the stags
honey from my lips keeps dripping
honey and milk are under my tongue
the smell of lebanon cedar is in my garments
my skin is a paradise of pomegranates
choice fruits henna plants and spikenard plants
sweet cane cinnamon frankincense myrrh
aloes and a spring of fresh water
clear cool water
let my perfume tickle the north wind
let the south wind come in to my garden
awake from your death my love
awake to me my love
you have run away my dear one
run away like a gazelle like a stag
my mountains of spices do not bring you back

*

oh jesus please
if you could bring my sibilius back
i would trade all that i have to you
all that i have for my pearl sibilius
i hold him in my heart and in my dreams
my body aches with loneliness
my body longs to be touched
if i touch and he is dead

should i hasten to my grave to join him
tell me should i seek a new man
a new man to marry and love
listen sheba fresh to my voice
you are a young childless woman
extend the love that is in you to a second husband
seek out your father to find a suitable match for you
go back to your father and start again
let us go now to sibilius tomb
let us smell his remains his dust
over his bare bones pray for his blessing
until the end of time he is with jah
there is a distant land where shaded forests hide
deep pools of reflected moonlight abide
he waits for you there by the seaside
his soul shines deep within your vision
your soul shines deep beyond my vision
your eyes are full of tears jesus
do you weep for me
am i looking for an eye embrace
is an eye embrace looking for me
my eyes regret never seeing sibilius
when i see your love in your eyes
listen to a song from the book of psalms
praise jah beautiful sheba
hallelujah to jah in his place of creation
thank mighty jah for his works of creation
commend the creator with the blowing of the horn
applaud the creator with the lyre and the harp
praise jah with the tambourine in a circle dance
celebrate the life of jah with melodious song
shout praise to jah with clashing cymbals
every breathing thing let it hallelujah
praise jah sheba and jah will show you the way
*

the last day with sheba i held a mirror to her eyes
told her to look deep within and she would see
sibilius holding hands with jah
she saw her departed love at peace
then sheba took the embrace of eyes ritual with me

the eye kiss led to a lip to lip kiss
the flower of a star burst in the sky
radiant colors flashing like ripples in a pond
it was hard to look away
on her finger I placed my ring
with a sigh she asked to marry me
this is not to be sheba
i am not the one destined to marry you
in this created world or the next
at the will of jah i will be a loving friend
remember my eyes fondness when i am gone
how can i forget the smell of your presence
it is the air after a rain shower
it is the skin of a baby in swaddling clothes
it is plunging my head in a an oasis pond
after crossing a desert
farewell sheba we remain united in the ring
*

VIII

with a letter from sheba to some of her freed slaves
who lived far along the coast at muscat
my boat departed the land of yemen
fierce long days on the sea alone
poor sam was sea sick
then my dolphin friends were companions
waves bounced in friendship
songs of dolphins cheered the sea
though the good days did not last
dolphins warned me of a ship approaching
bad colors bad voices they whistled
we moved into a cove on the coast
soon the ship spotted mine and came close
hooked onto my boat and came onboard
the men spoke a strange language
grey in tone grey and menacing with growls
they would not look into my eyes
many vile smelling men
they searched but did not find the hidden ring belt
a pirate took an axe and opened the hull
my boat sank in the shallow bay
onboard their ship the captain questioned me
their language too grey to understand
they chained me with other captives below deck
after two days of sailing the heat was cooking us
some of us began a drum beat music
all the slaves began to sing with me
a greek chant some had heard before
one boss who held a whip knew greek
he cracked his whip but did not hit anyone
we stopped and he took pity on us and gave out water
to each he gave warning of the captains wrath
that night in a quiet cove as all slept
the whip man perfedes came to me as a friend
as a fellow alexandrian
he pledged to help me

the next day in the afternoon a great wind blew
huge waves crashed over the sides
the ship began to take on water
the captain ordered the load lightened
perfedes unchained other captives not me
from the deck these men were tossed overboard
only four captives remained when the seas calmed
perfedes spoke in greek with me
these are the people of the night voices
a language based on feelings of hate
a language to obey as a slave
never shared companionship
their god is kali the destroyer
they sacrifice humans to this god
you are to be taken to their temple
it is on an island called astola
destiny will come to you at the kali maa temple
the captain again questioned me
perfedes translated my answers
both of their eyes were full of shadows
no eye embraces with them
where were you going in your little boat
to muscat to visit aristes and debante
why are you going what is your business
sharing the love of god is my business
then i told him the story of prince desmong
perfedes translated but the captain did not listen
all the doors in their eyes were closed
the captain had an icy smile
you must convince the priests of kali
when we land at astola tomorrow
from the dock we prisoners were dragged to a temple
locked up in cells with views of the temple
we watched many people gather for a ceremony
it began a few hours after dusk in the night
after the moon rose and shone above
perfedes was there beside the high altar
he was dressed as the high priest
he spoke and all the people bent down
torches were lit and costumed actors appeared

the drama began with a female four armed goddess
she slew two demons in an elaborate dance
then two actors carrying poles paraded
one with a snake on top and the other a crescent moon
up onto the altar a figure jumped
he was in a royal costume with a huge wig
there was a big eye painted on his forehead
the four armed goddess kneeled to him
he took out a two sided hand drum and waved it
the beaters attached hit each side
all the people pulled out drums and joined his rhythm
they chanted together
up above the altar
perfedes spoke in a loud voice
the people spoke back as a group chorus
two of the prisoners were dragged forward
and their throats were slit open
then it was over and everyone left
little sam came out of hiding
he had been a secret stowaway
his sharp teeth started work on parts of my bamboo cage

*

the next morning perfedes came dressed in a loin cloth
he told me what happened
the ritual is the goddess kali kills the demons
then two captives are brought to the altar
offered as sacrifices and their throats cut
the god shiva appears to bless the event
the skulls of the dead are used to make the hand drums
yes these people are now my people
alexandria offered me no power
the people here worship me
if you stay you can rule them with me
no it is not for me i told him
very well there is a role for you here tonight
he was hiding his eyes from me
late in the afternoon sam started chewing in secret again
after dusk sam and i slipped out
climbed into a small sailboat moored at the dock
shoved off and paddled out of the harbor

hoisted sail and veered north
towards the chariot in the sky and my star polaris
back to the cove i sailed
my boat still floated half submerged
diving in i found my hidden belt of rings
along the coast the dolphins found me again
we whistled in joy to each other

*

at muscat the slave aristes and his wife debante
welcomed news of their former masters
regretting the death of sibilius but pleased
that sheba was returning to her father
the tale of my capture and escape
gave them the opportunity to share tales
aristes was happy the island of astola did not claim me
happy also over my little friend sam
my news of sinai and two new commands moved them
they embraced all of my tales and truths
rituals of eye discerning colors of exact places
songs and psalms they learned and sang
my quest to the east on journeys of love
to explore friendship from person to person
to share lives link to link with ring symbols
aristes told of his contentment with serving
doing things for others as a way of life
debante shared the goal of a good slave
please the master with a smile for your work
obey the will of the master
if jah is the master of all
how do you learn what his will is i asked
this is why there is prayer i answered myself
a humble servant must bow down and pray
listen to the will of jah within
to pray is the way

*

when it was the day to depart
they asked that the little boat be left behind
the journey continued with their friend makkhali
aboard a large sailing ship as a crewman
heading to the port of krokola

near the mouth of the great sindu river
the place where alexander the great
gathered up his fleet after the indus campaign
their message of love in a letter carried by me
to jammu and his wife ravi
on this ship passage makkhali taught me
the language of the sindhi people
and shared some knowledge of the jain beliefs
he spoke of the vegetarian jain way
the practice of abstinence and chastity
give honor to all life all creatures even insects
jain stories of the wheel of life
the resurrection of the soul body
body to body reborn and reborn again
hindus as well as jains believe
depending on what you do in each life
you go into bodies of creatures simple at base
up to birds and smart animals and then as a person
many lives as a man or woman each time improving
progressing towards heaven or descending down
the chain becoming animals even insects
the reason why all life is revered
may be those birds those snakes those spiders
are reborn relatives in a next life
respect all life and you respect your ancestors
perhaps jesus in a previous life
your little sam was your grandfather
your belief in reincarnation makes me laugh
the moon does not get reborn as the sun
beings are born only once
one lifetime for all time to live fully
every genesis is being brave while facing the grave
*

in krokola i said farewell to makkhali
giving him a ring and an eye embrace color exchange
jammu and ravi took me to their home
they were weavers of wool from sheep
happy clothing makers for others
they eagerly introduced me to their friends
their fellow workers all freed men and weavers too

this was the clan way of life as a caste
many of their clothes were made for army use
a greek speaking military outfitter bought these
some romans had villas on the high ground
trading with army generals of the rajas of the east
society in krokola was confined to like to like groups
trades in common or points of view
the romans and greeks met at the baths
they exercised together at the gymnasium
jammu urged me to join in their activities
which the romans welcomed me into besides the baths
at the theatre there was work as an orator
sometimes as an actor on the stage
playing the lead in oedipus rex i was received well
oedipus who married his own mother
if i was a god
would i impregnate my mother
to make myself god
a son of god is not god
the annual monsoon rains came
as noah might have understood
water day after day water all night
not much to do other than weave wool
play as an actor on stage or play my new kitara
then one day a cobra slid in and swallowed sam in his sleep
unseen until it got stuck in its escape hole
with sam dead in its belly
my falling into despair for many days
led jammu and ravi to try to cheer me
jammu spoke of a higher spiritual clan of monks
of a loved master yogi named kalama
up river at a place called takker
a place of worship with a clan of spiritual leaders
enlightened ones on the wheel of life
intrigued and in search of wisdom
with a team of strong paddlers i went
up river to the temple at takker
the master kalama sat on a cushion
kneeling in front of him i held his hands
looked into his eyes for an eye embrace

the feathers of birds like wings closed
his eyelids hiding its nest
why hide your eyes master i asked
my speech is only for disciples
first you must take a vow of silence
yes he said i hear your mind agrees to become one
first take off all your clothes and possessions
second cut off all your hair
put these in this little wooden box and bury it
your old life must lay buried in a coffin
present yourself as a nude baby to me
take the simple robe that i give you
to wear as my disciple
eat only one bowl of grain each day
follow my example
listen to the instruction of your master
so i did as he bid
enrolled as his disciple
master kalama instructed every day
as a follower i learned his ways
he bent his body into different positions
holding each position focusing on breath
emptying the mind of words
he called this the yoga meditation
just single notes of music held as prayer
the way of yoga was devotion to follow
women were not allowed to follow
the men had vows of chastity
kalama let me play my kitara for an hour each morning
he listened and many weeks passed in the same routine
yet not once did he speak directly to my mind
my own approaches to his mind were met by ruffled feathers
the rainy season ended
master kalama sent us out in pairs to the farmers
to work in silence in the fields
after planting he gathered us together
he told us the way of yoga is from shiva
shiva is the god husband of kali
kali is the hindu goddess of death
light and life come from death he said

my mind rebelled at his words
the source of this way is darkness i knew
the island of astola was controlled by those gods
shiva and kali are both dark gods
false gods from darkness is not the way in
then kalama told us
that the world is flat like the back of a turtle
with an edge around it
the words of the greek thinkers in the scrolls
came to my mind aristarchus had calculated
that the earth was round in shape
the earth spun around the sun
the moon spun around the earth
all this in a sea of stars all around
my vow of silence was over
kalama your enlightenment
your thoughts are not the way in
the way to the creator is in harmony
with truth not superstition not dark gods
after this challenge to kalamas thoughts
my feet carried me back to the takker temple
dropping the robe i dug up my old being
from the wooden box i put on my old clothes
used my hair as a sash for the gold rings
and returned to jammu at krokola

*

IX

jammu welcomed my way in
my eye embrace found his eyes open and clear
tingling like golden wind chimes
he took my ring and sent me east
along the coast to a place named tisland
where his beloved brother sanjaya lived
sanjaya provided a room
this was a land without greeks and romans
here the caste groups were more separate
monks in yellow robes with begging bowls
strolled freely among every caste teaching all
men who spoke of the way of buddha to me
buddha means awakened or enlightened one
long ago a prince siddhartha gautama
after meeting a diseased man for the first time
then an old man and a corpse for the first time
this siddhartha saw the suffering in the world
he renounced his privileged life and became a monk
he set out to overcome sickness aging and death
first as a beggar then a yoga then an ascetic
he achieved higher consciousness through meditation
indulgence on the left path and denial on the right path
finally determining that a middle path is a better way
then he decided to sit under a pipal tree
he would sit until he found the truth
after days of meditation
he did learn the causes of human suffering
the four truths about human ways
first all things and states are unsatisfying
second we crave and cling to these things and states
thus we are stuck in an endless circle of death and rebirth
third if we stop craving and clinging to things and states
the circle is broken and we won't be reborn
fourth the circle is broken by even temperament
refusing impulses and desires

becoming mindful of the one being you are
entering a deep meditation state
transforming the self in the now
then siddhartha became buddha
this new being buddha entered nirvana
nirvana is the perfect peace of mind
supreme liberation
freedom from ignorance
freedom from greed hatred and defilement
no personal identity no boundaries of the mind remain
the tree he became enlightened under is the bodhi tree
it is still there at bodhi gaya after five hundred years
the people came to buddha seeking his words
that he reluctantly agreed to teach
the subtle deep difficult hard to understand
hard to grasp way to nirvana
buddha had many monks follow him
people from all castes
some were formerly nobles some slaves
some were formerly murderers
some women were formerly prostitutes
for forty five years buddha taught his way
finally he let his body expire
he became enveloped in parinirvana
buddha left the earth
then his body was cremated
veneration only to his words
the story of buddha fascinated me
i wanted to learn more

*

words are the wind blowing the way
the way led me to travel to the bodhi tree
there a group of women told me a story
after his own fathers death and deep meditation
buddha allowed women to become followers as well
he knew that they had equal capacity for awakening
as nuns they had stricter rules to shelter them
this was important as very few women were active nuns
men who kept domination states over women
such men are crippled on the path to reach nirvana

the true way will have equal women following
my memory of miriam sister of moses in scripture
made me see respect for women as part of the way
the prophetess miriam leading the women
with tambourines in dance
like buddha my voyage was along the ganges river
listening to teachers and learning stories
until i came to the famous bodhi tree
slept a moonless night under it
there i decided that buddhas story of a stuck circle
birth and rebirth was still a part of the hindu way
like odysseus stuck on the island of circe
lost in false embraces from the buddha and the jain
i needed the true north star to follow the right path
the true wain pointing the way in
*

continuing my walk along the ganges river
a path led to another sage master
who had a teaching about food we eat
food shapes being he said
the food eaten creates an energy of being
hindu regard for life grants only vegetable food
some say no flesh but fish from the sea
yet the creator feeds infants milk to nourish
elephant milk horse milk cow milk goat milk
are also taken in by people as creative food
consumed in the form of yogurt or cheese
to adults all curdled milk digests better
the claims of the benefits of milk are true
that elephant milk gives strength
horse milk running endurance
cow milk gives body growth
goat milk enhances taste
pure mothers milk is manna
each milk desired for its own nature the best food
vegetables first eaten by mothers pass into the milk
the wise consume milk before vegetables before fish
they never devour the flesh of living warm blood beings
more stories from other masters along the ganges
over many months passing rings to share friendships

sharing recipes of milk medicine and vegetables
learning how to make each kind of yogurt and cheese
my path through the country side
floating on a sea of milk
yet milk alone is not a god to worship
*

the words of the way in are like a flax seed
nourished by the milk of the soil
it grows and becomes many seeds
useful for oil useful for linen
oil to smooth digestion
words to smooth digestion of a way in
clothing to keep out the cold
words to keep out the cold of loneliness
*

wandering alone
surrounded by people
there was another city
a nameless city of strangers
too many languages that felt like babylon
too many people too many beggars
too much garbage too many flies
this nameless city also felt like jerusalem
too many holy men too many painted faces
people shouting for attention
people strutting like peacocks
all this crush of vanity
too many people pushing at me
mouths wagging at me
too many holy men looking for disciples
empty vanity creating temples for their beauty
temples full of mirrors of disciples
more teachers who strut for praise
it was time to keep the wain on my heart side
time to follow odysseus away from there
*

walking
under the stars
the road finally quiet
people sleeping in the city

building after building quiet
the world became less oppressive
then there was someone following me
a man had been a shadow behind me
during the day and all evening
was he a traveller going the same direction as me
now it was time to find out
stopping and waiting
who was he
what was he doing following me
he stood quietly and explained
just walking and fascinated by your look
you are a beautiful proportioned man
lean and lovely to look at
your smell leads me on your trail
my name is deap
may i walk with you for a while
so i walked with deap beside me
found myself telling him all about me
when i asked him anything
his answers were mostly one word
where are you from
village to village
what do you do
stonework
he was stout and very muscular
do you like wrestling
yes
then he reached in his satchel
brought out a chunk of buffalo cheese
gave me half to eat
followed by a swig of wine from his wineskin
we continued walking
it was too dark to see inside his eyes
his voice asked do you see the star antares there
the head of the scorpion
yes i do i said
then he put his hand on my rear
pursed his lips
can i suck your stinger

removing his hand laughing
no that is not my way i said
you should walk with someone else
yet he walked beside me in silence
suddenly pushing me into a doorway
swinging a short club from his satchel
which hit my shoulder as i ducked
grabbing at me with enormous strength
you will like it he hissed
in violence my body responded without thought
punching twisting and kicking
using all my wrestling moves in a row
escaping his clutches
then running hard
as he chased
until he was gone
an evil shadow man swirling behind
like a whirlwind that had tried to blow me over
his evil was in his desire to force himself on me
love only goes between two people
when both people want it
when it is on one side
it is power and pride
possession not love
*

X

reaching the mouth of the ganges
chittagong was a port at the river delta
looking there for a boat to leave
soon a sailor dashal a ring friend to be
found me at the port and took me in his boat
south across the sea to the island of tamal
we landed at a port kalutara
the island is another eden rich in plants
a full bounty of earth jungle greens
many vegetables in gardens of men as food
many herbs roots and barks with medicine power
groups of men sat with me in meditation
closer to the creator in prayer through magic plants
chewing leaves buds mushrooms and flowers
until a still point in the flow of time
provided vision of a third eye into the essence
of the material world as seen through spirit
a still point of silence

*

worlds of ants crawling in their cities
ants talking in smells with each other
growing the ant gardens tending their aphids
to provide milk as men get milk from goats
ants are in a smaller material universe
there are even tinier universes smaller than sight
living in tiny worlds on a finger tip
more universes than stars of heaven above
in my belly all living in harmony
tiny ants very tiny worlds the tiniest creatures
too small to see all living in harmonic song
little seeds grow into giant trees
the tiniest grain in my palm is as large as the sky
on tamal there were bags of seeds to collect
to carry with me to new lands
seeds of this eden to grow there

seeds of food seeds of medicine seeds of visions
lesson seeds from another eden this island
up a path there i climbed
towards adams peak mountain named there
climbing up seeking wisdom
meditating on a ledge on the mountain
in my sleep there in a dream a tiger came to me
a tiger named fire dance spoke to me
first in the cat body way then in my mind
the tigers voice came into my mind
you have the smell of the strange blood
your blood will stop up a flow quickly
wounds will not kill you like other men
your blood smells like an angels
jah god of all is teaching you how to live
that one is close to my angel friends
let us wait for the angel to come
under the gaze of the north star
that night in a dream within a dream
THE GIANT BIRD GABRIEL SPOKE GREETINGS
JESUS SON OF JAH
A VOICE IN HEBREW
TIGER THERE TOO IN CAT BODY WORDS
USE THE MIND WORDS TIGER INSISTED
THEN I HEARD INSIDE MY MIND
THE BIRD WORDS SPOKEN AGAIN
WE ANGELS HAVE WAITED FOR A SPEAKER TO COME
A HUMAN LEADER WHO CAN USE THE MIND WORDS
A TEACHER OF THE CREATOR
TO OVERCOME SATAN
IN THE MINDS OF MANKIND
TO RESTORE THE HARMONY
THE FLOW OF EDEN
THE LOVE BETWEEN ALL BEINGS
TO TEACH PEOPLE ABOUT THE OTHER CREATURES
IN THE WORLD
CREATURES ALL CREATED TO LOVE AND RESPECT
EACH OTHER
SOME OF US ARE OLD BIRDS
SOME ARE OLD TIGERS

SOME ARE ELEPHANTS
SOME DOLPHINS WHO CAN SHARE
THE MIND WORDS
THIS LANGUAGE THIS MESSAGE IS FROM JAH
THROUGH HIS MESSENGER ME
THE ANGEL GABRIEL
does the creator speak to you gabriel i asked
through you from inside the way
FROM OUTSIDE THE WAY
JAH OPENS OUR EARS TO MUSIC
OUR HEARTS TO SPIRIT
OUR EYES TO COLOR OF HIS WAY FRESH IN THE WORLD
OUR TOUCH GENTLE TO EACH OTHER
THE LOVE OF JEHOVAH IN EACH KIND OF CREATURE
GENTLE TO EACH OTHER AS FIRE DANCE IS TO GABRIEL
where does jehovah dwell i asked
JEHOVAH DWELLS INSIDE YOU
JAH IS WITH JEHOVAH
THE WAY IN TO LOVE
ON YOUR JOURNEY TO BE WITH JEHOVAH
THE LOVE WAY IS THE ONLY WAY IN
JESUS YOU ARE ON THE PATH
CONTINUE ON YOUR JOURNEY
JAH IS IN TIME BEHIND AND IN TIME AHEAD
MOST OF ALL IN TIME NOW WITH GABRIEL
UNDERSTAND THAT ANGELS ARE MORTAL LIKE YOU
WE ARE BLESSED WITH TEN TIMES THE POWER
WHEN HUMANS SEE THE LEAVES OF TREES
ANGELS SEE THE ANTS ON THE LEAVES
WHEN HUMANS HEAR A DISTANT BIRD SING
WE HEAR THE WIND IN ITS FEATHERS
WHEN HUMANS HAVE ONE CONVERSATION
WE HAVE TEN AT ONCE
EVERYTHING TO THE POWER OF TEN
YET YOU HEAR ME JESUS YOU OFFSPRING OF JAH
YOU ARE MORE THAN A MAN
CONTINUE YOUR JOURNEY AS A SEEKER
GO TO THE ISLANDS OF MALDIVE
DOLPHINS ARE WAITING THERE FOR YOU JESUS
OLD DOLPHIN QUEEN PING IS THERE

YOU HAVE MUCH TO LEARN
in the waking morning i was alone
gabriel had taken wing
fire dance had prowled away
it was time to heed the words of the dream
*

from port kalutara with dashal in his dhoni boat
with my sack of seeds and my ring sash
we sailed for many days under a hot sun
arriving at some islands
the islanders there called themselves dhives
hundreds of islands one known as male
where men live to trade with outsiders
keep strangers away from the women dhive
male is where i left dashal to set sail back
only men in male but as a harmless monk
the dhive men took me in
on other islands the dhives have women rulers
held in the highest honor
wise women watch over warriors
leaders at peace not war
the oldest and most humble are queens
with palaces beside the waves that they know well
white sand beaches coconut trees they dance through
in the turquoise waters the old queens are loved
fishing the abundant sea
diving for oyster pearls
pearls too from giant clams and sponges to trade
seeking the precious and the practical
dried fish coir rope especially cowry shells
these shells are used as coins
given to their men at male for trade
the women move from island to island
avoiding outsiders
men who seek to rape
men who kidnap
all evil men
this is why traders find only men at male
the dhives only allow trade at male
keep distant those possessed of satan

those who resist the natural way of the sea
taught to the dhives by the queen dolphins
at one island i was met by queen ping
the oldest queen dolphin
into the water with her forehead to forehead
more a mind embrace than an eye embrace
ping echoing through the halls of my mind
diving with her and riding her back
leaping over waves i felt like a child again
her subjects brought me then to the women
queen ishta of the dhives had some glass lenses
fashioned into things to keep the water out of the eyes
with these one can see the ocean creatures as if above
the ocean bounty of myriad life the women swim in
leaders such as queen ping taught the humans
first their language then their ways
all of these beings worship the creator
the creator as womanly mother of all
the greatest lesson of mother is silence
quiet service to others my mother mary taught
dolphins rounded up fish to feed the humans
they showed the groupers the snappers the barracuda
the lobsters the eels tuna and shellfish to eat
puffer fish and lionfish to obtain poisons to use
small amounts to heal
large doses to kill dangerous beings
predators like the reef sharks even pirate men
bad men from the great satan world
honor the older wiser women the dolphins say
let them lead by example the way in
queen ping faced me in an eye embrace
a row of nude dolphin queens were in her eyes
like the apparitions in augustus eyes
these noble ancestors were revealed
the queens of the sea for eons of time
swimming in the dark waters of her eyes
speaking softly and sweetly singing
for many months i lived and learned
diving into the reef waters of love
diving into the dark ocean of sleep

keeping my mind from constant swimming
turning towards the things i could not see
feeling the emptiness inside me
for the dolphin i cannot be
the shadow of my mother
the silence of my sleep
the silence of my dreams
the shadow of my leap
in the coolness of the ocean
in the silence of the deep
the voices of the mind asleep
the shallowness of my kind swimming above
these dolphins sing of an angels love
these beings sing with the love of a dove
the dolphin tribes hear angels and they love their words
wisest gabriel knows all the languages of all the beings
calls each dolphin by name
when gabriel calls out the same
they herd the fish to feed
angel power for wings in need
gabriel sings songs to them of the way in
the presence of the creator in the sea of sin
only weeks before a pair of the angels had been there
telling dolphins to make the way ready for jesus to stay
is gabriel in a real team and not simply a dream
when it is time to be jesus will really see

*

queen ishta told me a parable
a story to plant in my mind garden
if you are asked by your child for a fish
would you give your child a serpent
let holy words of love
go to those who know jah
wolves may come to you in sheeps clothing
yet you can hear the howl in their voices
their secrets in their eyes
turn them back outside
keep what is precious away from wolves
keep pearls away from swine

lest they tear and trample these
turn on you next to do the same
people are like the plants on the earth
you will know them by their fruits
there is no gathering of grapes from thorn bushes
there is no gathering of figs from thistles
good fruit comes from good plants
good deeds come from good people
plant good seeds in people
*

queen ishta and ten of the older dhive women
all joined in eye embraces
received golden rings of friendship from me
queen ishta and queen ping prepared a boat to sail and sing
with dried fish to feast and provisions to travel east
taking me in a boat towed by dolphins afloat
they each took turns pulling without rope burns
the whales of the deep gave directions to keep
to the dolphins of the time of smoothest waters sign
the quiet skies the longer time made short by stronger
powerful dolphin fish showed me love to wish
over oceans deep and silent shores steep
resting at bays to restore our days
a soft wind blowing for a sacred glowing
leaving laughing in song and landing lovingly along
dolphins took me there to a new shore bare
*

humbly landing in a new unknown country
walking overland across an isthmus
an easy journey to an eastern coast
friendly faces along the road
a farmer offered a meal and a bed
that evening he gave me mushrooms
mushrooms to open the world
outside to flood the inside
held back by the senses
words became living images
thoughts of the never seen before now
connections and flow from jah

drifting dreams of cloudy skies
in the mists of morning
the farmer pointed north
the path led me to a master teacher
a man called sing a master of a ring

*

sing chanted om mani padme hum
om mani padme hum
repeated
sing said that consciousness has four realms
three living realms waking meditation and dreaming
finally the fourth the realm of death
death passes through a succession of five states
earth water fire air and space
consciousness in earth is attention and focus
in water consciousness is flexibility and creativity
in fire the state of emotions goes from cold to hot
in air consciousness grasps concepts quickly
air relates these into abstract ideas
consciousness in space is openness wide relaxation
dying is the dissolution of each element
first earth dissolves into water
the body is weak and shrivels
the eyesight blurs as though seeing a mirage
everything is yellow and earthquakes are felt
then a thirst for water like a tidal wave
smoke comes into the vision as fire comes
thinking fades as all turns red in an inferno
breathing becomes heavy as fear eliminates smell
the action of dying is then air dissolving to space
breathing stops the tongue is thick no taste
green turns towards white as the wind blows
touch has gone as energy dissolves
consciousness of the body has gone
into the space of the universe
sing says the song may move through the elements
in an hour or in a day or several days
just as every night that one goes through sleep
one can awaken so it is with the death process
a master can awaken to consciousness three days

after most of the elements have dissolved
the buddha gave a parable of consciousness departing
the day of death is like a herd of cows
the door to the barn is opened
the strongest will lead the others first
if no cow is strongest then the old habit
leader will go first otherwise
the one next to the door will go first
if none of these move then
the cows will all try to get out at once
practice letting the elements die
then the selfish body may fade
a warm light of compassion can begin
consciousness of helping and benefiting others
awakens the spiritual warrior in you
striving to be more open caring and loving
then the mushrooms and food of space
became puzzles to solve as sing showed answers
mushroom melodies
this one with the red cap may kill
this one is the oyster of land good to eat
here large brown caps best cooked
and here the bells growing on cattle dung
these are the sacred mushrooms of visions
god gives these as the way in
with a pocket of the mushrooms
ideas and songs from master sing
one less golden ring took me further
*

XI

arriving alone at a village of bankok
people with a new look
slender and soothing serene souls
dancing the women wore long fingernails
accentuating the flow and connection
a movement of celebration in silk
like birds fluttering with chirping voices singing
every note a world within a world
joy and laughter tears and fears
it was like the people of congo singing again
a different tune yet a familiar tune
a celebration with higher notes
children all children of jah

*

east and north the way was deep forest
alone up a path to meditate
a lake with a turquoise color
the color of love to sit and dream beside
men were nearby making noise chopping trees
an old man came riding an elephant dragging a log
his rope broke and he asked me to help him retie it
again it broke and he fell off the elephant
hurt from the fall
too exhausted to remount so he sat beside me
my name is natapong phong
he was surprised to hear me respond in his language
jesus is my name what is your elephants name
ronarong
is ronarong a follower of buddha
silly man he is a follower of natapong phong
we laughed together and the elephant laughed too
tell me your story and the words flowed
rivers of friendship rivers of the way in
then his story of forest life
my daughter niki will be along to help me .

soon a young woman came on another elephant
dragging her own log and hearing us laugh
she leaped off her elephant and came to her father
why aren't you helping him you joker she said to me
he never asked me to ride ronarong
you are not smart enough to ride an elephant
natapong said get up onto ronarong and show her
the guiding language was easy
ronarong wanted to play along and laugh
she pulled the log to float with the others
gathered at the shore before us
natapong introduced his daughter niki phong
get off that elephant before your ears are boxed
she was delightful in her tough manner
spitting words out of her beautiful mouth
full lips and straight white teeth
sparkling eyes she demanded how my eyes
had the color of lake nanboon
my reply to her beauty and fire came
how are your eyes so green as the forest
and so delightful above your rosy cheeky cheeks
take my hands and look into my eyes deeply
your eyes have water of the lagoon color
as well as green forest like the eyes
in the tail feathers of a peacock
if you two can break off from each other there is work to do
my ankle is twisted daughter let him drive
all that day niki led the logging
natapong gave an evening meal and played drums
niki danced with long fingernails and flowing dress
not for me she said just for practice
it was for me and then niki sang a voice perfect
there was no stopping falling in love
a love complete as soon as it formed
with niki a woman perfect peacock eyes
love grew like feathers fanning fully

*

a wedding celebration and a feast followed
music with all the elephants dancing too
a song that ronarong stamped her feet to

this is the song i sang for niki
there is a time when time is gone
that is the time when i am with you
there is a place that is the centre of you
there is a place in the centre of you for me to be
two shall become one together
oh niki my niki my love
your voice sings like a light warm wind on my ears
the notes ring as bells inside my ears
your smell is a distant rose on that wind
the bee in me must find the nectar
oh niki your sweet nectar fills my mouth with joy
the perfect place where i belong
there i see your color blends with mine
bright in the golden love of jah
we touch each other softly
the touch of jah joins us
two are one together in jah
there is a time when time is come
that is the time when i am with you
there is a place where we circle each other
then the sound that vibrates our souls
where the smell that draws us together
the taste of you on my lips and in my mouth
niki and jesus two gold rings
perfect pleasure together
our touch together perfect pleasure
love touch forever together
love touch forever

*

in the verdant forest we worked together
side by side on the elephants
there at lake nanboon our logs floated
our perfect place to play and sing
a duet of love in the flesh
let the lord in you love the lord in me
sweet seas in your eyes softly sigh
skin shimmering on legs strong sinuous
nuzzling the nape of your neck
lean and lithe luscious lady

you send a shiver up my spine that spreads
touching your tree trunk thighs
bouncing on your beautiful bumble bee
let your long hair loose and laugh my love
my lion lay against my length
move your mouth in my mysteries
together our tongues touching tasting
opening oysters for pearls to possess
collecting colors creating our children
growing greetings to golden gods

*

children coming
soon the belly of niki grew
we brought twins into the world
our son adam our daughter eve
this was eden for niki and jesus
happy heaven on earth
wilawan the sister of niki weaned her older child
she lent her breasts to provide more milk
precious mothers milk for adam and eve
until the twins were two years old
weaned and ate other food

*

we played on the beach at lake nanboon
our children then three years old
perfect beings full of our love
adam tossed in the air please papa higher
he played with a pet monkey climbing trees
a beautiful boy of boundless energy
eve beautiful in a bright yellow dress
her pet peacocks pretty beside her
a darling daughter dancing in delight
as a mother niki was the nourishing earth itself
as a father grace and love were smooth steps
we lived in a glowing golden white globe
the kingdom of god is a garden of eden
cultivated within our minds bodies and souls
we are gods gardeners
we have seeds of goodness kindness and mercy
seeds of love to plant and grow

in the spring of our youth the light of god
warms our earth and the seeds sprout
our plants grow in sunlight and moonlight
even as we sleep the garden grows
the water of love and care nourishes
small kindnesses are drops of rain
each day we judge which plants stay
which plants are unwanted weeds
pulled out to become compost food
for the good plants of the mind
our body is a garden of eden
the soul of god makes us gardeners
cultivators growers creators
a heartbeat blooms as a rose
your laughter is yellow hanging bell flowers
the work of our grass brings us bread
sweet apricots mixed in the dance of love
figs full of seeds to teach our children
the smell of lavender songs

*

my niki has words like a distant flute
her unseen hand pulls my heart to a clearing
she is the promise of a warm hearth on a cold night
she smiles like a young girl her teeth white pearls
her skin is silver white in the moonlight
her hand stirs the water in a pool
it glides graceful as a dancer
her long hair is a shadow behind her
she sings a magic song with eyes dark and curious
her mouth in a wide dangerous smile
with bright sparkle laughter
her other hand holds her saucy hip
swift as a sparrow i dart across the meadow
she bounds away as graceful as a deer
giving chase i leap after her
niki runs as a child light and quick without fear
in her wake the smell of her earth shines
the grey of the moonlit stones flash like stars
as she dodges me waits again for the brush of my touch
skips away flicks branches to spray me with dew

a warm dew in my hair as she pulls me close
her mouth is eager her tongue shy and darting
a sigh of warm breath of a clover meadow
her hot tips of breasts pressed against my chest
her smell is like ripe apples on the ground
my hands are on the back of her neck
they slide on her smooth skin the length of her thigh
they grab her hard on her flank
circle narrow waist lift her lie her down
writhing beneath slow and breathy
her legs wrap around me
her back arches as her hot hands clutch my shoulders
she bites my arms and digs nails in my back
astride me as a rider her movements galloping wildly
her long hair whips as a mane
a great tremble
the earthquake shaking as she cries out
wordless cries rising and falling
our racing hearts slow from frantic thunder
to the half heard thumping of distant drums
my body is a lute a trembling string too tight
the world stops and all of me arches
above the flower petal of her mouth
her eyelids flutter like butterfly wings
above the rich colors in her eyes kissing mine
traces of gold on green on blue and black
my strings roar like a tiger and snap
we are one in a bolt of lightning
a flash of light melts our bodies into one
blue green and yellow flash like lightning
strike my heart and i want to die
then we fall to sleep in each others arms
niki moves in sleep murmurs in sweet breath
her round hips her slender legs her soft breasts
watching the lean muscles of her belly ripple
she awakens and stretches like a cat
in the sun beside me stroked to the tip of her tail
she looks at me with eyes as intent as a bird
are you a stag in rut her lips pout
my kiss is as a feather tickling

towards the birdsong of morning
*

above us a noise to remember
the chatter of a wounded monkey
suddenly the monkey fell from a tree
blood pouring out of every opening
a sickness bled it to death
too sudden too soon too slippery
our garden was on fire with pain
we ran too sickly too silently too slowly
our children so near so far
then alpha adam fell bleeding too
and eve omega moments later
both crying in pain
at the day the night the hour the moment
dead in our arms
in an instant time stopped
*

the night came with no moon
the dark night came too soon
darkness with no pillow
darkness darkness all cold below
take our hearts and let them bleed
take the silence and let it feed
there upon my bed
i felt the hair upon her head
the glow across her face
i saw the lightnings trace
i heard the thunder
the blood out of your ears
my blood that was tears
and i felt the thunder
our children lost beyond alarms
my niki lost from my arms
an empty kiss the taste of blood
empty words to stem the flood
and i cried the wonder
the blood of niki in my arms
darkness darkness take away the harms
no lightning in her eyes

no answer for my cries
there is the distant thunder
on the night with no moon
the elephants began to weep
the trumpets filled the forest bed
darkness darkness my loved ones dead
*

the elephant trunks reached to touch
my dead loved ones and time stopped
oh jah what have you let happen to me
why jah why these deaths to this jesus
this man tore at his hair weeping blood
this jesus threw earth at the sky
why jah why is my niki dead
why jah my alpha and omega are dead
take me now and kill me
my life is no more oh jah
what have you let happen to your jesus
this is more than any man can bear
my blood poured out but i did not die
weak in bed too weak to rise
feeling flashing fires feasting
hearing the fires burn my loved ones bodies
all the people wailed
all the earth wailed
jah did not answer jesus
jah was not there
this is the end between us
oh almighty jah goodbye
this is my end a grain of sand
a very tiny grain
at the back of my throat
a circle ring of memories of faces
other grains of sand looking at me
as the wind of my breath rose and fell
in the tube of my throat
a great canyon in front of the grain
falling inside the grain of sand itself
into a space that was dark
dark and empty with just the rush of moving

dark time vast distances between points of light
as stars rushing in the sky falling
the comet of my golden grain
passing a red sun a blue sun a green sun
a dark green essence of niki
there the purple core in the centre was adam
alpha my sun my only son
there was a whirling blue glowing dot eve
glowing omega circling the core
all my force dived toward them
all my rushing crashed into them
this is the end an explosion of color

*

i woke up on my bed
living not dead empty
jah would not let me go
days passed as i lay quiet
wilawan the sister of niki came to me
she forced soup down my throat
it tumbled in the tunnel in front
of the grain of sand of my being
there at the back of my throat
do not die jesus she prayed over me
then natapong came and sat weeping
you are to blame jesus for these deaths
allowing my daughter and grandchildren to die
why did you not protect those in your care
my answer the will was there not the power
why did you not call on your god to save them
jah would not answer me
why did you live and they died
jah would not let me die
what is the purpose of these deaths
questions jah would not answer
take the rings back that you gave us
here one from my finger
our friendship is over
here three from the funeral pyre
from daughter grandson and granddaughter

XII

there were voices without speaking
my mind heard the wind
words flowed from the air inside my mind
mind to mind thoughts
did i hear the wind of gods mind
a storm of images thoughts sensations overpowered
a tiger told tragedy tumbled out of time
the words of fire dance the tiger came from the wind
the voice in the wind spoke
the monkeys began to bleed and die
the bats in caves bled and died
the bleeding disease came into the world
it moves from bats to monkeys
then men who are too close to monkeys
tigers avoid eating these creatures
disease lingers in the blood we smell it
you have it in your blood smell jesus
the odor is faint it remains to protect you
tigers and leopards and lions will avoid your flesh
the pain of this knowledge shook me
why had i allowed adam to play with the monkey
monkey disease too close to adam
*
in silence the forest called and the wind calmed
empty echoes of my family all gone
wandering on the back of the elephant
riding ronarong rumbling deep
deep in the forest beside a pool
the elephant bowed down in prayer
this is the graveyard of my kind
leave me here and ronarong left
i was the bones alone
beside the waters of death
lonely bones

*

a white tiger came
real in flesh
the tiger lay down in front of me
my name is sheama
staring at me intently
are you going to eat me
no the tiger shook its head
you are not a fish it said
cat language in my mind as i looked at the tiger
even as you understand me in throat sound
mixed with ear twitch eye blink head nods
small movements nose wrinkles toe flicks
all the signs and signals for us to communicate
you teach when your mind reaches for me
this mimicking like your echo returns to you
when we face each other like mirrors
use sound and movement like dance
when we are close our minds meet
we communicate directly without words
without body movements
white tiger and man
you and i become one being
can you eat yourself no
why are you here and what do you want
tiger answered in the cat tongue
directly into my mind
jah sent me to rise up in you
to give you strength
you are cast out of this eden
the dead eden of wife and children
time to follow me
the promised land is not here
you must follow me
the tiger eyes shone as she spoke
bright emerald with flashes of blue and gold
niki eyes i saw in sheama
niki was in her
no she is not in me sheama said
the wind from jah says you are to follow me

bury the three rings here
the ring of niki the ring of adam the ring of eve
give the natapong ring to wilawan
take the remaining fifty six rings
you must come with me on a journey east
make a boat for us to travel up the great river
we must go up the mekong to china
this white tiger once lived in china
sheama hears herself echo
echo back to her home in china
*

nikis elephant took us to the river run
a great tree brought down by natapong
for me to hollow out as a boat long
into the boat and onto a river called mun
at one end sheama lay
while i paddled during the day
at night sheama swimming would tow
while i slept laying low
behind the boat a baited fish line
provided food for us to dine
the slow flow of the mun downstream
met the mighty mekong and we turned upstream
past unknown villages along the shore
some pretty porpoises played alongside
river dolphin talk to share more
along with cautions of crocodiles beside
sturgeons and swimming snakes galore
*

the melody of memories mingled
as each paddle stroke brought jah to mind
sheamas mind merged with mine
ALL TEN OF GODS LAWS ARE SURPASSED BY TWO
LOVE GOD AND LOVE OTHERS AS YOU WOULD YOURSELF
sheamas voice answered mekong means my king
some people worship the river flowing by
love me jah your river with your whole heart
with your whole soul your whole being
if i love you jah will you love me
will mekong jah bless my river of life

THE FIRST OF THE TEN COMMANDMENTS FLOWS BY
THEN THE REST OF THE OLD LAWS
*
does jah live in all the air all the earth
all the sea all the rivers sheamas mind asked
THE SUN THE MOON AND THE STARS
true idols are silent and dead i tell the tiger
little images like in the old tabernacle of abraham
childish dolls are to laugh about
why must i worship only one god she asks
THERE IS ONLY ONE GOD I AM WHAT I AM
why does i am call itself jah sheama asks
with a thousand names are all names holy
every name part of you is a part of me
then cursing jah is cursing yourself you say jesus
so if i call you a rat i am calling myself one
that is the rat way to let the mind obey
my friend sam was led that way
the way in to jah is quiet balance you say
with the weight of time slowing the pace every day
clear of distraction we are floating and pray
the vessels jah uses to create you are your parents
parents are two hulls below your deck
love the vessels that carried you to your awakening
avoid the rock words that may puncture your hull
share in creation honor yourself as a creator
honor yourself as a mother and a father
honor your children and they will honor you
jah will keep your boat afloat
if he chooses you sheama adds
even as he drowns your wife and children
jah claims to be a creator of life a lover of life
why have life to live forever when all beings die
THE WAY TO LIVE FOREVER IS TO BECOME A CREATOR
then suffer the death of your children created
in time with jah where is the room for death she asks
creating murder will distance time i answer
does jah murder turning away from sick children

murdering myself to join my loved ones
do the bonds of a couple hold fast in death
if you love jah and extend this love to a partner
your partner in love creates a new eden with you
the two as one are a song a dance to jah
together now is together always

*

give all that you have to others
let others give to you freely sheama says
barter this for that if you have needs
if everything comes from jah freely
why not just take it sheama asks
ask only for what you truly need
the asking is a way out from jah i say
is the commandment for truth telling the way in to jah
false truths are stumbling blocks on the way
let your words be true in your stories
your stories are witnesses to be recalled
at the end of time
even as death is the end of your story
at the end of time this is your story jesus
those told of others will be truly told
as in your story of me told to jah
let all the beings all the things you desire
float beside you on the river of the way to jah
putting too much in your boat will sink it
too much weight to satisfy your desire
too much to satisfy your need
to be at one with jah
why is every seventh day a rest day
does the river of time flow strongly for six lengths
on the seventh it is slow and full of eddies
the creation river could just as easily slow down
every three days or nine days or ten days
the thoughts of ten between jah and mankind
are all contained in the two new commandments
love jah first and all mankind as yourself
what of other kinds who share our world
not rocks nor trees nor insects nor fish

all of us warm blooded creatures
a third new commandment from sheama
love other warm blooded beings as you love your own
there is another new law the eleventh
learn from the other animals
as well as the birds of the earth
learn how they communicate with each other
love other intelligent beings as you do yourself
*

yes you are sunshine on my soul
paddling up the mekong
with my friend jesus
up the river of life
both of us nurtured by fish
our minds merged
as we looked deeply
into each others eyes
always go deep sheama said
you should have plunged deeper into mothers eyes
you should have penetrated the defense
in the eyes of the deap man
the power is in your will
how do tigers worship jah
love other creatures as you love yourself
*

several weeks upriver a group of warriors
surrounded us in boats and waved spears
sheama roared at them and they shrunk away
violence fades when surprised she said
we must hurry along
before they become familiar
travelling together but avoiding people
who might be afraid at seeing a tiger
*

the mind of sheama read her story
when i was young a prince of china raised me
all of his court grew used to seeing me
sheama the white tiger became friendly to all
all the court smelled friendly

yet an assassin stabbed my prince as i slept
this tiger failed her prince
sheama exiled herself
wandering lost and alone for a year
until you found me jesus
you are my new prince just like my old one
just like i look like your niki
we echo each other
yet when i looked deep into tigers eyes again
sheamas eyes were bluer than nikis were
why had i seen niki in this tiger
sheama shared more of her life story
my parents were captives of the emperor
living under the whip of cruel trainers
in an enclosure at the capital chang an
as a kitten i was taken from my mother
becoming a gift for a prince to raise
the grandson of the xiongnu king huhanye
his grandmother the beautiful wang zhaojun
said to be so stunning that geese fell from the sky
at the sight of her riding her horse
this prince yituzhiyashi the second
fed his tiger fish and only fish every day by hand
now i have no taste for anything other than fish
the prince loved me and called me sheama
i loved him back but even his death
even in revenge i could not kill
before jesus he was the only man i understood
the prince made me a free princess of the palace
the servants would bow to me in worship
dressing in silk drapes as i strolled
the tiger stroll is a kind of dance
sheama showed me to her own purr humm
the prince taught you a private language
it is one that you have shared with me sheama
the tigress and i danced together
in our minds we danced together
*

mountains rose up steep beside the mekong

at times the boat was dragged along the shore
when the current was too strong or rapid
the mountain cold penetrated the water
tiger needed to come out and warm up every hour
my arms ached with the effort of paddling
we made less and less progress against the flow
one day upstream past a merchant dock
tiger hid on the shore and our boat was traded
nets for fishing a rain tarp clothes for me
a cart trail beside the river led forward
night was our progress
to avoid people we slept during the day
under our tarp
sheama wrapped me in soft fur and warmth
licking me affectionately with her rough tongue
the grey stripes on her white fur had darkened
too much sun even in the shade for her snow
which had become creamy white along her back
with my strokes she purred as i admired her
echoes face her niki echo eyes
her front had no stripes
her sides and especially her tail were marked
the tail was my guide hand in the black night
she could see where i could only hear
finally a place where sheama had first come
to the mekong over a pass a few days journey
from the valley of the great yangtze river
the road east to mother river of china
*

soon we walked beside the yangtze at night
until finding a suitable boat tied up beside a hut
sheama hid in the forest for a few days
while i made friends with the man in the hut
a man with a simple name lee
his eyes a simple brown
his place the same inside him and outside him
learning his language and playing music for him
this man opened his heart to me
near a place called panzhihua

a ring of love for him and a boat gift to us
he was quiet when sheama joined for fish dinner
he held her paw and kissed it as we departed
*
down the yangtze we floated along
repeating the day and night routine
only rarely paddling or towing
liangshan is a good and kind place
again a warm welcome to my strangeness
sheama hiding in a forest while men visit
enjoy a meal of vegetables and rice
good beer and funny faces
downriver we cruise through yibin
then past luzhou a convoy surrounds us
too many boats and people to avoid
sheama roars out but no one is afraid
many bow and begin to pray
sheama is their goddess come home
we have an empty net from all the chanting
into bodao city where the fish market
finally provides food for a hungry tiger
men approach me with reverence
the escort prince to the great sheama
they tell me that we must go to the emperor
from zitong a noble retinue grows at mei
a royal procession for queen tiger
we are put in a coach and pulled along
by military men riding rhinoceros
beasts like some i saw in africa
it was strange to see them ridden in a parade
followed by one hundred chariots
beautiful horses and great lords
to the gates of the capital chang an
*

XIII

through the palace
to the temple of heaven
at the centre
only the emperor knows shangdi
this is the jah god of china and he is high priest
the only mortal allowed to speak to god shangdi
the jade emperor along with the sun and moon
above the clouds rain and thunder
sheama is in white silk i am in a blue robe
we approach emperor guangwu who asks us
do you claim to be an emperor too like fan chong
let me warn you that all the pretenders are dead
the red eyebrows are gone and warlords too
you come from where gongsun shu is rising up
no i have come from lands far to the west
joining sheama we came up the mekong river
in china we came down the yangtze
we have not heard of gongsun and know no warriors
people call me a prince of peace
yet i am only a student seeking learning
sheama he said belongs in the palace gardens
this is the tiger raised by prince yituzhiyashi
does she still only eat fish or does she eat meat now
choose your dish he pointed to the offering table
sheama ate the fish and didn't touch the meat
you will live with the pandas who only eat bamboo
they will not eat you and you not them
as for you jesus you may live beside them
and study at the rujia school of scholars
your life at the palace is to advise me
and accompany sheama when she is required
here now emperor guangwu
look into my eyes
hold my hands i tell him
feel my presence and hear my words

let our eyes embrace and visions in them be revealed
you are a warrior aware of dangerous rivals
many will rise up against you but you will defeat them
this is what my god jah has revealed to me
my god and your god shangdi the same being
behind the names
peace will be in your realm while my time is here
peace from heaven at this study time
yet my gift to you is to create art in your empire
you will appoint me over all the artisans
all the musicians dancers and performers
all the animals and birds and their caregivers
we shall create beauty within your palace
the presence of beauty will strengthen you
warriors will want to protect the beauty
merchants will want to provide goods to it
farmers will want to contribute food to it
the heart of the empire will be art
this will come to be in one year
and then i will depart
you are welcome to do as you say prince jesus
this emperor sees heaven in your eyes
feels the warmth and love in your hands
hears the beauty of the words spoken
*

the school had a master teacher tao
named after the book tao te ching
written by the old master laozi
tao taught the sage wisdom of kingship
from the five visions books of kong qiu
the yin and yang of gamble time in the i ching
rhymes and rhythms of ren on how to be real
sayings and speeches of the true sovereigns and sages
the rites of merchants artists scholars and farmers
stories and sensations of the spirits of old
ren is love other people
the same golden rule that i understood
treat others as you want to be treated zhong
yi is love of fair play and yi is kindness
with the virtue chi knowing right from wrong

li is love of leading the right dance steps
with goodness liang and proper respect gong
zhi is love of contentment of knowing right
yet humbly with rang and bravely with yong
xin is love and compassion for yourself
with xiao respect for your elders especially kong
the master teaches virtues with shu forgiveness
these chinese teachings were satisfying
good ways in towards enlightenment
*

the emperor called me to a council of advisors
on an evening of the new moon
a time neither yang or sunny
nor a time yin full moon
the emperor had a dialogue on a book
the yellow emperors inner canon book
discussions about human vitality and life force
the world the cosmos and balance
what must be done for the yin and yang balance
to keep the emperor and the empire healthy
my first observation is that the people are ill
too much love of money and gambling
the fault is the nature of number names
two is easy and bright auspicious pairs
four is bad luck death the same word sound
eight sounds like wealth or fortune
five is like not or lack of something
the sound of seven is to leave or grow out of it
the emperors number nine is everlasting
gambling is getting good luck avoiding bad
this language meaning of words creates luck
what would happen if new names were given to numbers
new sounds that did not sound like other words
number words that are neutral simply numbers
the emperor decided against my suggestion
he decreed that tradition must rule
gambling is good entertainment for the people
*

at a second meeting of the emperors council
my question was why the yin or the yang

why is the sun yang and the moon yin
why is the yang hot and the yin cold
why is yang upward and yin downward
the emperor said the yang is male and the yin is female
no answers to my whys
the emperor simply smiled wise
then my question why is everything five phases
either wood or fire or earth or metal or water
these phases make sense as colors
red for fire
yellow for earth
green blue for wood
maybe white for metal and black for water
but the phases are nonsense directions
why is wood east fire south metal west
water north and earth the center
why do we see the wood or taste fire eat earth
smell metal and hear water
the emperor answered your wood is sour
your fire is bitter your water too salty
your earth may be sweet but your metal stinks
you ask too many questions jesus
go and create art
*

master tao taught me the sayings of laozi
these i memorized
those who know do not say
those who say do not know
without darkness there can be no light
if you see something as beautiful
other things become ugly
if you judge some people as good
other people become bad
the way is like water it benefits all life
water does not compete with life
try to change it and you pollute it
try to hold it and you lose it
water stays in lowly places that others reject
the main concept in the laozi teaching is wu wei

wu wei means flowing with the moment
wu wei in action is without effort natural
wu wei comes when you are empty of desire
master tao was like his name
powerful yet humble
tao is the source the root of all things
one of his disciples began to follow me
a young man named judu see
now i take no disciples i told him
if you wish to be a follower of mine
in a few years take the silk road west
some of the emperors cloth is mine to give you
take it for trade
when I return to jerusalem wu wei
then and there you can become a disciple

*

the emperor called for his doctors and me
my vital energy my chi is low he said
my appetite is lazy my tongue is fat
my face is pale and i sit and sweat
what is wrong with me and what do i need
one doctor told him acupuncture
to rebalance his chi plus ginseng for energy
artemisia for his sweating and fir moss
to fend off senility
what i am not a crazy old man
leave my presence you fool
another doctor diagnosed his health
as lack of sex drive and the emperor nodded
you need to eat the testicles and penis of a dog
also the penis and the horns of a stag
the gall bladder of a bear will bring color
strength can come from tiger bone soup
but best of all rhinoceros horn
this made me see red and black
do not listen to that man my lord
my advice is it is all in your mind
nothing that you take will help
animal parts do not cure at all

plants and herbs may help for a moment
take your mind off your body
let your imagination fuel your energy
wu wei is what you need
stay away from food until you are hungry
run around the garden until you sweat
this will bring color to your face
your manhood will rise naturally
when your empress dances perfumed and light
then let wu wei carry you along
so be it the emperor agreed with me

*

at the gardens i asked sheama if she knew other tigers
yes just before we met a tiger prince tried to seduce me
he was not a big enough tiger to impress me
males want to dominate rather than share
he left me with his ear torn like others before him
if you were a tiger jesus it would be a marriage
but until you become one i remain a virgin
her eyes were intense blue not at all like nikis eyes

*

musicians and singers came from all over
a new kitara was fashioned for me to play
leading others with kitaras horns drums
the instruments to support the singing
to accompany the dancing and drama
there were many large painted panels
all the produce of the empire represented
all the flowering trees fruits and nuts
all the birds and insects drawn large
the panels were strung and floated as flags
bits of scenery around the performance area
the main plaza for thousands to gather
to enjoy the beauty of the performances
animals joined in the movements
horses dogs monkeys pandas and all sizes of cat
including the biggest rhinoceros
bigger elephants and sheama in the heart of it
peacocks doves roosters and owls were there

masks costumes hats and pendants were worn
many flowing dyed silk gowns
new art created day after day for a great crowd
it was just as tiberius had said
feed the mob
give entertainment and they will love you
*

a tiger king joined in from the north
like sheama he had been taken as a kitten
he had been raised by a princess
fed only fish and called fire king
he did remind me of old tiger fire dance
the mind to mind words of sheama
did not work when i tried to talk to him
he does not wish to talk with you jesus
both animals must want it for it to occur
this fire king tiger did set sheama ablaze
sheama was blessed to marry him
finally she found one worthy to love
we staged a wedding feast to celebrate
thousands of new people came every day
the empire had counted fifty million people
every person wanted to come
those invited brought gifts
half their goods for an invitation
no taxes when gifts are so rich
my year climaxed with a celebration
the emperor thanked every member of our troop
he bid me farewell from his empire
blessed the bag of seeds from his palace garden
as i gave him a ring of friendship to remember me
he gave me an invention he called a pointer
a glass toped tiny box with an iron needle
suspended at the centre always pointing north
that is where prayers to shangdi go
when you travel you will always know the direction
emperor guangwu also gave me a ship with twenty crew
to sail and row to wherever i wanted to go
*

first to cipangu
also known as japan
there to visit the kinai and yamata people
gentle soft spoken and very polite
a family people also followers of kong qui
see no evil hear no evil speak no evil do no evil
do unto others as you would do to yourself
all respecting each other and their elders
yet in cipangu
disturbing worship shrines to the dead
idols of ancestors and other gods
too many idols and too quiet gardens
there was no god like jah no shangdi
shrines to gods of the forest
worship of mountains
nothing to learn that brought true happiness
the people too aloof
to hug and jump
the yamata were too shy
to laugh and play
they liked to fish
one day i followed
some fishermen down to the coast
there was a natural harbor being filled
by men out at sea driving fish in
setting a net at the mouth of the inlet
to trap the fish in and spear them
they drove a group of dolphins in
drew the net and guarded it
tossing spears at any dolphin who tried to escape
these people wanted to murder dolphins
screaming at them to stop
then calling a dolphin i dove in
calming their panic my mind reached out
a dolphin made contact and came to me
listening he let me ride his back
like the sea horse trick of my youth
we circled to the astonishment of the yamata
then we led the pod to leap over the net

*

later i called a meeting with the yamata lords
told them that emperor guangwu decreed
no dolphins are to be taken
it is forbidden
they nodded yes
liars behind their smiles

*

after one month my ship sailed north
then east past aleutian peoples islands
forty days of stormy seas along a coast
great trees and rainy skies for many days
plenty of fish to eat and new villages to greet
some large black and white dolphins
leaped beside us and scared the sailors
when i called to them in dolphin words
told them that the men were afraid
that they would swallow them
carry them for three days
like the prophet jonah
spit them out on a strange shore
they told me that was a lie
no whale would or could do that
they guided us south along a heavy forest shore
for three days

*

XIV

we met a people called kwakutal
this people lived in lodges
behind huge wooden statues
not idols they said not worshiped
these images told stories reminders
real animal and bird ways
carved on their totem poles
there were these gods these thunderbirds
not gods they said they were real
bird men visitors every year
beings who spoke their language
ate their fish their salmon from rivers
thinking of these beings as monsters
my sailors wanted to return to china
so it was farewell to them
the kwakutal took me in when they left
the simple village life
learning the language
a man called laughing loon befriended me
loon was a shaman master of ceremonies
a big celebration was coming soon
he asked if i would join his musicians
there were three people practicing on drums
my beating was fourth following along
the celebration was a potlatch
feasting gift giving and healing
a big potlatch
laughing loon joined me in an eye embrace
his dark centres were like deep pools of water
surrounded by dark bark they were the hearts of trees
out from this trunk radiated lighter brown branch roots
in an intertwining pattern looping cords
between the cords were a circle of backs of fish
dotted backs with specks of orange and red
swimming to go between the roots

into the water pool tree centre
a mysterious image
*

hosted by chief dan of the village
hundreds of people arrived in canoes
at a potlatch the greatest honor is giving
everything that a village has is given to others
chief dan presented all their stored food
enough feasting for three days
until nothing is left
on the first day there was a good welcome ceremony
stories around the campfires
with our beating drums
people dancing in circles and singing
the chief giving out presents and food treats
on the second day chief dan did an eye embrace
my eyes kissed the vision in his eyes
it was sparkling stars in a deep dark night
there is the sun on water in your eyes he saw
the stars in your eyes are in a pattern
like orion the hunter i told him
when the sky got dark i pointed out the stars
of the belt of orion
chief dan saw three otter pelts hanging from the belt
a warm winter coming he said
later on the second evening
loon staged a show
with a group of costumed and masked characters
a sick man was placed on a board at the front
loon entered dressed in a thunderbird costume
he danced around and produced carved images
figures representing the sick man one after another
each figure smaller than the last until a small one
was put on a string necklace as loon held up a paddle
he moved as if he were in a canoe
bumping into a shore he got out
as if a hunter stalking around an island
looking here and there
suddenly two monster characters jumped out
this was much like the kali show at astola

loon proceeded to overpower and defeat the monsters
from each monster he took a stick hand
to fit on the sides of the doll figure
loon then got back in his magic canoe and came back
with much fan fare
loon placed the whole doll in the arms of the sick man
who rose up and joined in dance
this was a ceremony of a journey
to the island of the dead
a masquerade
to capture the sick mans soul and return it
simple magic hard to believe
still good at heart and far from satan
the third day the feasts continued
but all the guests complained with exaggeration
too full bellies no more
that night under a huge mother tree
dried cactus flowers peyote buttons were passed out
loon told me buttons were traded from the desert people
very bitter and an hour later causing vomiting
loon sat beside me closely in a small group
he touched my male parts with a caress
no loon i told him i am not that way
after the drums became soft and distant
another awake vision came out of the fire
every particle from the flames sparkled
flashes of color dots swirled through eyes
the very air like water all around alive
living dreams took shape as phantoms solid
new words to understand new ways
memories of many beings
came firm awakened
queen ping floated in the air as if in the sea
elephant ronarong trumpeted behind me
turning there was niki on her back
holding the twins adam and eve on each side
my tears flooded
my eyes dissolving the vision
the fire sparks in the smoke buzzed like insects
loon said your spirit helpers are coming

leaping up a tree limb i began to climb
halfway to the top i met a raven
it looked at me with deep eyes
cocked its neck why are you climbing
was it my imagination talking
no it was reading body language
it flew away and i looked at the fire below
there was no reason to be in the tree like a bird
so i climbed back down and sat beside loon
my bird gave me my name he said
the moon was full above us
i heard a wolf howl
the voice of the wolf demanded an answer
a power a compulsion seemed to come over me
onto all fours i bounded into the forest
from the shore my voice howled back at the wolf
we seemed to be talking about a hunt
the urge to hunt like a wolf took over
my vision and especially my sense of smell were sharp
beside a trail i came upon loon
shivering in fear don't hurt me
i am a deer
leaving him there
my being released of the wolf force
sitting again at the fire loon came
holding a bear cub
what are you doing with that little cub
the baby is mine to cuddle he said
there was a noise of branches breaking in the dark
a heavy grunting angry black bear came closer
give her back her cub i told loon
there is no way I can leave her he said
grabbing the cub i tossed it to the mother
the bears left
loon began to sob
that was my totem animal my helper
dawn came as our group sat in a circle
each chanting a prayer
the world itself reflected through them

peace be with you
all was still as i found a place to lay down
under the arms of a great mother tree
when i awoke i was alone
silent
the potlatch was over
*

a few days later i was paddling alone
along a coast beside a forest
the tide came and a strong current pulled
my dugout canoe fast
a strange sucking sound was ahead
the whole ocean dipping down
draining into a hole
the water moving in a circle
a log was falling down the swift swirling drain
that will be me in a moment i thought
as i paddled with all my might
to break out of the rushing flow
around the outside of the circle once
then around again as the centre roared
it gasped for me
like the mouth of a mountain swallowing a river
praying for more strength
my paddling was like wings beating furiously
slowly escaping on the third circle around
then shooting like an arrow along the shore
racing terror in my heart
when i came ashore safe
my thoughts settled on the parts of my mind
that the drug from the peyote buttons
the mushroom mists
the hashish visions
had swirled around dangers as well
in the sea waters of the mind
*

XV

a ring to chief dan and another to loon
salmon fish filled the rivers
swam up to spawn signaling time
the salmon heralded the thunderbirds
the kwakutal people expected them
only one bird arrived
one thunderbird is more than enough
it spotted me and flew down to me
a truly magnificent creature a great bird
multi colored feathers with bands of blue green
red and black a white face with a small bill
bright intelligent eyes mine in a mirror
a wingspan equal to five men stretching arms
taller by half than a man standing
with feet bare with talons like an eagle
but very flexible like hands
it spoke to me in the kwakutal tongue
MY NAME IS GABRIEL IT SAID
WE MET IN DREAMS BEFORE JESUS
NOW IN THIS REALITY I HAVE COME TO YOU
you are speaking to me out loud i said
yet at the same time in my mind
like sheama the tiger
YES THERE IS BOTH
BUT ONLY BECAUSE YOUR MIND KNOWS HOW
ONLY A FEW MEN HEAR THE MIND VOICE
SHARE THOUGHTS WITH ANOTHER BEING
YES JESUS THE ANSWER TO YOUR QUESTION
DOLPHINS CAN HEAR THIS WAY AS WELL
it is like praying to god you say
ANGELS ARE NOT GOD
WE ARE MESSENGERS GABRIEL SAID
IT IS TIME TO GATHER YOUR SEEDS
BRING YOUR RINGS
a simple command to obey in my mind

first I need to look into your eyes
THIS IS THE FIRST TRUE EXCHANGE
YES JESUS MY EYES ARE VERY REAL
visions of rainbows rise up in the blue sky
CLIMB ABOARD
*

riding on the angels back
wings soaring
we flew over mountains
landing on the top of one
the angel spoke in my mind
gabriel shared a history
about the flock of angels
WE CAN LIVE FOR OVER A THOUSAND YEARS
SOME HAVE LIVED NEARLY TWO THOUSAND YEARS
FROM A NEWBORN IT IS TEN YEARS BEFORE FLYING
ONE HUNDRED AND FIFTY YEARS FOR FULL GROWTH
THEN WE MAY MATE
THE MOST PROLIFIC HAVE ONE YOUNG
ABOUT EVERY FIFTY YEARS
INTENSE LEARNING OCCUPIES THE FIRST HUNDRED YEARS
FOR THOUSANDS OF YEARS WE WERE THE ONLY BEINGS
WITH CONSCIOUSNESS OF THE CREATOR GOD
SOME MALES OTHERS FEMALES LIKE ME
ONLY HUNDREDS OF US ON THE PLANET
OUR MISSION TO GUIDE OTHER BEINGS
TO HIGHER CONSCIOUSNESS
THE DOLPHINS AND WHALES WERE FIRST
THEN ELEPHANTS AND MANKIND AND OTHER ANIMALS
DOGS HORSES PARROTS APES TIGERS
MANY KINDS EACH WITH UNIQUE CONSCIOUSNESS
PERCEPTIONS LANGUAGES WAYS OF BEING THOUGHTS
WE ARE TRAINED TO ENTER THOUGHTS AND DREAMS
DROP SEEDS OF IDEAS
SET DOMINANT PATTERNS
EVOKE STRONG EMOTIONS
SHEPHERD THE WHOLE WORLD OF CREATURES
LEAD ALL TO THE WAY IN TO THE CREATOR
YES JESUS IT WAS ANGELS WHO INSPIRED RATS
AT ALEXANDRIA

THE FIRST COMMANDED RATS TO EAT CERTAIN SCROLLS
THEN A SECOND INSPIRED RATS TO LISTEN TO DAVID
SAVE YOU FROM SLAUGHTER
YES JESUS THERE ARE TWO FLOCKS OF ANGELS
JAH IS THE LEADER OF ONE FLOCK
SATAN IS THE LEADER OF THE OTHER
SOME ANGELS LIKE ME TRY TO KEEP PEACE
AGED BEYOND HAVING YOUNG
OUR ROLE TO BECOME MESSENGERS
AMBASSADORS BRIDGES BETWEEN FLOCKS
BETWEEN PEOPLE TOO
AT TIMES I HEAR PRAYERS AND SPEAK TO THEIR DREAMS
YES I DID SPEAK TO YOUR MOTHER MARY
BEFORE YOU WERE BORN
BUT ENOUGH OF THIS TALK
THIS AMBASSADOR IS BRINGING YOU TO ANOTHER ANGEL

XVI

then we flew again
silent all night in the wind
arriving at a lakeshore before dawn
far along the lonely shore
a fire appeared
as we came down i saw another angel beside it
this one hunched over a fire
bigger than gabriel
feathers glistening flashing colors darker hues
like oil on dark water in sunlight
the three of us spoke in our minds
THE FISH ARE ROASTING ON THE FIRE
THE DARK ONE SAID
YOU KNOW I EAT MINE RAW GABRIEL SAID
raw or cooked is fine with me i said
TAKE YOUR PICK THE GLISTENING ONE SAID
we ate in silence as the sun rose
MY NAME IS QUETZALCOATL
LEAVE THE MAN WITH ME GABRIEL HE SAID
moments later i was alone with him
YES JESUS MY FEATHERS ARE BEAUTIFUL
quetzalcoatl shared my thought
as the sun rose
we looked into each others eyes
his were shimmering green waves
into deep pools of water
over dormant volcano mouths
GET ON MY BACK HE COMMANDED
we flew all day south
crossing rivers and deserts
at dusk he landed along a lake shore
we quenched our thirst
MAKE A FIRE HE TOLD ME
giving a spinning cord and stick from around his neck
he flew out over the water

scooped up a fish and brought it to me
then another larger fish for himself
as we ate
in my mind he answered my questions
WE ARE GOING TO MY GREAT TEMPLE
PEOPLE THERE ALL OBEY MY MIND
WE DO NOT TALK THEY LISTEN
THE REASON YOU CAN MIND TALK
YOU HAVE ANGEL BLOOD IN YOU
YOUR MOTHER MARY IS A DESCENDANT
OF THE ANGEL JAH
ANGELS CAN BREED WITH MANKIND
THEIR CHILDREN LOOK LIKE MANKIND
THEY HAVE NO WINGS
BUT THEY HAVE MINDS THAT TALK
THESE HALF BREEDS ARE USUALLY BARREN
LIKE MULES FROM DONKEYS AND HORSES
BARREN EXCEPT FOR THE ODD FEMALE
YOUR MOTHER WAS A DESCENDENT OF THAT TYPE
YES JAH IS AN ANGEL
THE PRESENT JAH IS THE THIRD JAH
JUST LIKE SATAN IS THE THIRD SATAN
THE MANTLE PASSED DOWN THROUGH THE AGES
YES JESUS I QUETZALCOATL AM FROM SATANS FLOCK
NO WE ARE NOT GOING TO HIM
YOU ARE A VERY RARE MALE DESCENDENT
A CURIOSITY YES
THE REASON THAT I AM TAKING YOU
IS TO SHOW YOU THE WAY IN THROUGH THE MIND
TEACH YOU AND READ YOUR THOUGHTS
AS WE GO

*

we continued for five more days
my power to stop the conversation
to stop his mind from entering mine
astonished him
YOU HAVE MORE POWER THAN MOST ANGELS HE SAID
YET YOU DO NOT KNOW HOW TO MIND TRAVEL
OVER LONG DISTANCES
in the morning we passed over a tall mountain

before noon we stopped at a lake
quetzalcoatl looked back north and asked me
HOW LONG WOULD IT TAKE YOU ON HORSEBACK
TO TRAVEL BACK TO THAT MOUNTAIN
ten times as long as we just flew
I WANT YOU TO STAY HERE
LOOKING AT THAT MOUNTAIN
WHILE I FLY BACK THERE IN HALF THE TIME
WITHOUT A BURDEN LIKE YOU TO SLOW ME DOWN
YOU THINK OF JAH AND PRAY IN THAT DIRECTION
WHEN I GET THERE I AM GOING TO KNOCK
ON YOUR MIND DOOR
IF YOU LET ME IN YOU WILL BE TAUGHT
DISTANCE VOICE MIND TALK
so it was
the attitude of prayer travelled the distance
the mind tuned like a bell
like a flash of lightning
the colors of speech
flew
*

QUETZALCOATL TOLD ME
THE MOTHER OF AUGUSTUS
THE WOMAN ATIA IS LIKE YOUR MOTHER
SHE IS A DESCENDENT OF THE ANGEL SATAN
AS MARY IS OF THE LINE OF JAH
YET HER SON AUGUSTUS DID NOT HAVE YOUR ABILITY
YOU ARE A NEW KIND JESUS
A MYSTERY
A VERY NEW CREATION OF BEING
*

we came to his city and his temple
he set me on a lower pyramid
ordered servants to bring me food and water
quetzalcoatl bid me to listen in on his talking to the people
it was a one way speech
the thousands of people were like ants
the warriors presented dozens of captives
men women and children marched up the stairs
to the stone altar

one after another they were killed
hearts raised up still beating
quetzalcoatl was a god over them
a basket of hearts was brought to him on top
DELICIOUS HE SAID TO ME
MUCH TASTIER THAN FISH
IT IS A PITY YOU DON'T WANT TO TRY ANY
ECHOED AS MY MIND SHUT
*

guarded by a ring of warriors
quetzalcoatl fell asleep
before dawn my mind heard men whispering
a large group of warriors had crept up the side of the pyramid
they overpowered the guards as quetzalcoatl woke
to a barrage of poison tipped blow darts
he looked surprised
HIS MIND ASKED ME TO HELP
but my mind had sent help to the rebels
mental blocks to help them
overcome the bloodthirsty god
*

blood begets blood
the soldiers proceeded to skin the corpse of the angel
their leader wore it as a mantle
with a mask carved like the face of quetzalcoatl
he had learned the trick well
shutting off his mind first to the god
now to me
this man proclaimed himself god
ordered more captives to be sacrificed
it was time for me to leave
quickly
at the east coast of the sea
the gold cup of the dead god was traded for a boat
paddling north along the shore
after a day I spoke out to dolphins
mind chatter
they scooted me along
*

three dolphins joined my mind flow

pulling on my bow rope tow in turns
ringee loved to turn circles
flipkee jumped out of the water
twisting and flipping
zanee sped through waves
zinging and singing
ringee flipkee and zanee
they told me of a tussle
two factions of angels
each speaking dolphin words
with their minds
just like you do jesus
most of us like the jah angels
some of the bigger whale dolphins
the black and white ones
choose the satan side
jah tells us to love other animals
all the warm blooded creatures
do not kill them
do not eat them
satan tells the big brothers that they may eat
the weaker minded ones
like walruses seals
porpoises sea otters and even big whales
but none of us kill humans
fishermen sailors and swimmers
we are pulling you to some islands
we call bahamas
the angel gabriel asked us to do this
*

XVII

by starlight
on an island beach
looking at the wain group of stars
focused on polaris
my mind prayers to jah were sent
JAH SPOKE TO ME
AS HE SPOKE HIS VOICE RANG LIKE DAWN LIGHT
IT IS NOT YET TIME TO MEET FACE TO FACE
WHEN YOU PRAY ALL THE ANGELS HEAR US
YOU HAVE MET SOME OF THE FLOCK OF SATAN
AS WELL AS THE MESSENGER GABRIEL
YOU HAVE SOME GIFTS
DEEP SIGHT PENETRATING PRAYERS
YOU MUST GO BACK TO YOUR HOMELAND
TEACH MEN WHAT YOU HAVE LEARNED
LEAD THE WAY IN FLOCK
IT IS AN ODYSSEY
AFTERWARDS
YOU MAY COME TO ME
FACE TO FACE
EYE TO EYE
COLOR TO COLOR
MIND TO MIND
GABRIEL IS SENT TO YOU
GO WITH HER
*

gabriel returned to me
why did you take me to quetzalcoatl i asked
HE HAD A MOST POWERFUL MIND LISTENING POWER
HE COULD TALK FROM VERY LONG DISTANCES
YOU LEARNED TO RESIST HIM IN HIS WORDS
BY LISTENING NOW YOUR OWN POWER WORKS
MOST ANGELS NEED TO BE WITHIN SIGHT TO HEAR MINDS
YOU JESUS HAVE MORE ABILITY
THAN ANY PERSON BEFORE YOU

YOU MAY GAIN MORE IN TIME
most people can be known
but lack the ability to know
that reminds me of the saying of laozi
YES I HEARD THAT ECHO IN YOUR MIND JESUS
SATAN SEEKS OUT EVERY BEING THAT CAN MIND TALK
HE HAS A VOICE AGAINST THE ANGEL JAH
SATAN SAYS THAT HE DOES NOT BELIEVE
THAT JEHOVAH EXISTS
IN THE REALM OF THE LIVING
HE ONLY HEARS THE VOICE OF JAH
satan is the father of the lie
EXISTENCE IS CONSCIOUSNESS SO JEHOVAH EXISTS
EVEN IF HE IS NOT SEEN
JAH ASKED THAT I TAKE YOU BACK
TO YOUR HOMELAND
THE PROMISED LAND
*

days and nights flying
resting when tired
finding fish to eat
unless the sea below was vast oceans
the north star always guiding
the iron needle pointing the direction
gabriel flew then towards the north
we landed on an icy island
without people
the pointer needle spun in circles
we entered a cave halfway up a cliff face
deep inside it was a warm resting place
a warm pool of water to soothe my body
gabriel spoke
THIS IS A HOME OF THE NORTH STAR
SPIRIT PRAYERS OF MEN TO JAH COME HERE
THE PRAYERS FOLLOW THE IRON FORCE POINTED HERE
THIS IS A PLACE WHERE ANGELS HAVE EARS
can i send back answers if i hear prayers
WHEN YOUR SPIRIT DWELLS HERE WITH JAH
TRY IT JESUS
ARE YOU CONNECTING

WITH THE PRAYERS OF ANYONE
yes i hear my mother mary
my mind hears her prayer
she is happy that i am alive
she wants me home
ANYONE ELSE
yes many voices many prayers
IT IS NOT YET TIME FOR YOU TO ANSWER THEM
FOR MYSELF I HEAR JAH LISTENING GABRIEL ADDED
BUT HIS VOICE IS A FORCE
DIRECTING ME NOT SPEAKING DIRECTLY
*

let me pray to jah
please hear my mind calling
then an answer
JAH SPOKE TO ME
YOU ARE MY ANOINTED ONE JESUS
LISTEN TO ME
THERE HAVE BEEN THREE ANGELS CALLED JAH
MY GRANDFATHER WAS THE FIRST
MY FATHER WAS THE SECOND
NOW I AM ALIVE
THE FIRST AND SECOND LIVED
NEARLY THREE THOUSAND YEARS
GRANDFATHER TRANSFORMED AT DEATH INTO JEHOVAH
HE BECAME CONSCIOUS AS THE CREATOR
FATHER ALSO MERGED WITH JEHOVAH
ON THE DAY YOU WERE CONCEIVED JESUS
THAT DAY I BECAME JAH
MY PREDECESSORS EXIST AS JEHOVAH
NOW I AM ONLY TWO HUNDRED YEARS OLD
THE OTHER ANGELS SHELTER ME FROM SATANS FLOCK
NO MAN HAS SEEN ME YET
ONLY YOU JESUS ARE COMING INTO MY PRESENCE
IF YOU COMPLETE THE TASKS AHEAD OF YOU
AFTER YOUR DEATH I WILL RAISE YOU
BACK TO LIFE
ALLOW YOU TO BECOME MY RIGHT HAND
IN MY INTERACTIONS WITH PEOPLE
THE TEN LAWS OF JEHOVAH WERE GIVEN TO MOSES

TO TRY TO COUNTER SATANS SEEDS
SPREAD IN MILLIONS OF GRAINS OF WEEDS
IN MENS MINDS
YOUR TASK IS TO PLANT NEW LOVING SEEDS
STRONGER PLANTS TO OUTGROW THE WEEDS
ALL OF SATANS SEEDS ARE SELFISH IDEAS
HE SAYS ALL GODS ARE EQUAL
WORSHIP ANY GOD YOU LIKE
WORSHIP THROUGH IDOLS IF YOU LIKE
CURSE GODS WHO DO NOT HELP YOU
EVERY DAY IS A STRUGGLE
THERE IS NO SUCH THING AS REST
CAST YOUR PARENTS ASIDE AND BECOME YOURSELF
KILLING OPPONENTS IS THE SAME AS WHAT
ALL THE GODS DO
TWO INDIVIDUALS NEVER MERGE AS ONE
HAVE SEX WITH WHOMEVER YOU DESIRE
TAKE WHATEVER YOU NEED OR WANT
TAKE FROM THOSE WHO HAVE MORE THAN YOU
LIE IF YOU HAVE TO
JEALOUSY IS NATURAL
TAKE FROM PEOPLE BETTER OFF THAN YOU
TURN THEIR BETTER FORTUNE
THEIR BETTER THINGS INTO MOTIVATION
TO GET MORE FOR YOURSELF
THESE ARE THE SEEDS OF SATAN
DO YOU UNDERSTAND YOUR TASK JESUS
yes i do

*

we left the cave and flew onward
crossing huge islands
crossing dark seas and great forests
then south across seas of grass
lakes and rivers dry desert sands
until finally reaching mount sinai
JAH MAY TO SPEAK TO YOU DIRECTLY AGAIN
HERE IN THIS LAND HIS VOICE IS STRONG
WHEN IS SOON ENOUGH GABRIEL SAID
as we landed there on the top of mount sinai

JAH HAS ASKED ME TO LEAVE YOU HERE ALONE
WITH MY PROMISE TO MEET YOU AGAIN JESUS
in my mind i heard in forty moons time
near the temple of jah in jerusalem

XVIII

on my feet walking again
the promised land beckons
behind the nabateans lands
there came the dead sea
at the oasis ein gedi some jewish scholars
essenes shared bread and scrolls in a temple
ascetics like buddhist monks caring little for food
searching for the true way of jah in words of isaiah
also in false scrolls of the twelve patriarchs
men convinced of the doom of israel at roman hands
messiah will lead the resistance from masada
messiah seed of david will triumph over rome
essenes will join him when he takes over masada
our messiah will come as a conquering king
will you join if messiah is a prince of peace
that is what the scriptures say he will be
no the prophesies call for a warrior king like david
peace will come after the war is won
what if messiah comes as a woman i ask
the essenes rise as one
that is sacrilege
women are not leaders of gods people
no i say what is down may come up
the future is not the same as the past
what is unknown will become known
jehovah is what he will prove to be
down the road lies jericho
joshua does not have to blow the trumpets again
*

up the river jordan
a crowd was camped
followers of john the holy prophet
dressed in sack cloth eater of honey
john preached

go to the east bank
wander in the wilderness
for forty days and nights
remember moses and the people of israel
entering the promised land a people of jah
repent your sins you unworthy tribe
beg jah to forgive your sins
immerse yourselves in the purifying waters of the jordan
enter again to the west bank
as a chosen person
a blessed follower of the only god jah
you are baptized holy again by the waters of the jordan
then you can enter the promised land
as a member of the flock of jehovah
john greeted me
cousin jesus
you are as ragged as i am
bearded and rough like a shaggy lion
just the sort to be a wild man like me
dip your feet in the jordan and follow me
what do you prophesy cousin john
messiah is coming
no john messiah is come
the people are not fit to receive messiah
the messiah is come to those fit and those unfit
are you the messiah jesus
you yourself are witness john
continue to baptize and cleanse the people
you may baptize me as that is your way
those who follow me recognize me
in time you and your followers will know me
now my mother waits for me in nazareth
mary has not seen her son in over ten years
*

on the way to nazareth there were wild animals
held in a compound and crying their doom
tigers and lions destined for slaughter in rome
in the night we spoke and they were set free
given directions and cautions to avoid men
lions to egypt tigers to the far east home

my way in regards to wild animals is love
the way in to the wild being inside oneself is love
*

the purchased land james farmed with my mother
my sisters and brothers supported a flock of sheep
james was a carpenter like his father had been
a good man welcoming his long lost brother
like a prodigal son deserving another chance
yet jesus was not destined to be family head
only a visiting loved one knows how long to stay
gifts for each of them the seeds were planted
that were in my pack
for a new garden of eden
that my family would cultivate
the new garden of many plants with healing ways
food and spices and medicine plants grew
as well as other seeds from my stories
of the journeys
that the way had taken me
*

after an embrace of eyes
lazarus was glad to have some new plants
to add to his many medicines and treatments
five years before he had married my sister hanna
in their household they also had his sisters martha and mary
as well as the very excited to see me again
wonderful warm and wanton nana
squeezing me in her embrace
as was her way
she loved to follow lazarus and hanna
a helping nurse to the physicians
we visited the sick and injured together
lazarus cut out growths bound and stitched wounds
gave plant potions to cure fever and rashes
when the sick were mind weary or possessed
it was my turn to lay hands
gaze into eyes
bring happy color back
with love and care
we seeded some mushrooms in dung

from dung the flowers for the mind grew
lazarus told me that tiberius had sent him messages
delivered by soldiers to him in secret
even though lazarus had told him
he wanted nothing from him
nothing to do with him
tiberius persisted and vowed to force him to rome
using family and friends as hostages
if he would not come
he did steal our horses back
golden eye and lucifer
they were shipped back to rome
*

lazarus exchanged stories with me
he told me of his adventures
while i had been away on mine
two years after you left he began
living in this villa that i purchased
you noticed the large courtyard with high walls
that is nanas favorite spot
a protected place for her to retreat to
when we were home on rare occasions
we were mostly gone
practicing as healers throughout the country side
nana loved to give hugs
sick and depressed women responded to her touch
my work was more practical
fixing broken bones and stitching cuts
giving potions and healing medicines
my life was happy until we were suddenly surrounded
captured by a whole century of soldiers
sent by tiberius to bring me to rome
along with my horses and any family
my sisters were not found
but i told them nana was my daughter
she was quick to massage the leader
back in rome tiberius wanted to order me about
nana humored him and delighted his court
she was dressed in a toga with jewelry

like a noble roman woman
of course it was a mockery of them
a comedy like the bawdy theatre
that tiberius really enjoyed
naturally his mother livia hated us
she had a slave girl take care of nana
instructed this gwen that was her name
to poison the bono in her food
nana is not stupid and she smelled it out
gwen fell in love with nana
so i took the opportunity to escape
gwen was a druid princess from gaul
this is where we went
me in royal dress with a fast carriage
who would stop a relative of the preceps
right up to the front garrison in gaul
then on through forests in the land of picts
gwen led us to her village
*

the leader of the people was a druid priest
an old man named allanon
he was known as a prophet
his helper was a boy named mug
we settled in with them and allanon
agreed to instruct me in how to live
as a healer in the land
allanon had a treatment to cure leprosy
he used sulfur from a hot spring
dirt from a pine forest
with the afflicted having urine sweat and tears
turn orange indicating effective treatment
using medicine from plants and the earth itself
different diseases were cured
*

the druids have a spiritual path
a way in understanding
that is passed along by word of mouth
it is forbidden to write it down
he taught that there are spirits in everything

even rocks and trees
people are just a thread in the web of life
live and die and get reborn
allanon talked about the otherworld
that people visit in dreams and go to after death
a resting place for souls
that you come back and are reborn from
a druid isn't really much of a priest
they say they only have a little wisdom
that is their quest wisdom
they spend a lot of time meditating
in sacred groves in the forest
they also celebrate the bards and poets
singers of sagas
mostly about tradesmen and crafters
druid priests call themselves peace makers
the forest groves are peace groves
they really hate roman soldiers
men of mars who eat bread of anger and bitterness
*

nana and gwen and i stayed with these people about a year
then mercenaries from tiberius
bounty hunters began to arrive
the first one was captured by the village folk
they have a fall harvest festival
allanon judged this man as a betrayer of his people
this roman mercenary was bundled up in a suit of branches
they called him a wooden man
paraded him about on a cart
some bards sang songs around a big fire
then they lit the wooden man on fire
to them it was their natural way
they ignored my objections
*

gwen and nana and i went to a small hut
in the forest away from the village
to hide from any other bounty hunters
allanon told me a story of a priest who sought wisdom
he went in search of inspiration
a treasure of enlightenment found in three drops

he and his apprentice searched the wide world
for many years but could not find the fountain
the old priest lay on his death bed in his cottage
it was raining outside
on the priests death the apprentice went to the doorway
felt a thirst and held his mouth up to the drips from the roof
three drops hit his tongue
he closed his mouth
he knew what to do
*

then i went back to rome and saw tiberius again
he was living in a villa on the island of capri
he ranted like a madman along the bluffs
very jealous and alone
his agents brought his supposed bastard children to him
seeking comfort in young sons and daughters
servants told me that he threw some off the cliff
they were judged unworthy
it was disgusting to be near tiberius
he had a skin condition perhaps leprosy
that he tried to hide under masks he wore
using knowledge from the druids
led me to make a medicine to treat him
as a reward he let me go back to judea
take nana and get her married off he said
then come back to me
there are no other bonos to marry her to
it was too far to go back to her homeland
so we stayed happy here in galilee
and i am the one who got married off
to your beautiful sister hanna
*

in nazareth there was a happy wedding to attend
my brother jude was to be married
at the feast the wine ran out
but the day was saved
lazarus knew how to draw the essence from wine
boiling and cooling vapors to draw out power
in liquid that appeared as water
that ten times mixed with water

would thin back to wine
he had the foresight
to bring four jars of it
we poured the liquid of lazarus
into jars of water
the wedding celebration continued happy
my mother and the whole family were delighted
the bride and groom my brother especially
everyone began to dance
my sister introduced me to a girl lene
a slim and sensuous seventeen year old
mary of magdelene town
called lene as so many other marys were near
including my own mother mary
lene held my hands and looked into my eyes
a recognition struck me
her left eye was a color like nikis eyes
her right bluer like sheamas eyes
each eye different from the other
both eyes again haunting blue green gold and brown
they reminded me of peacock feather eyes
lene looked i love you in her mind
her smiles were true
yet deep inside there was a secret shadow
my mind probed her hidden memory
a dark menacing shadow
like the man deap
had caged her with fear
as a young girl resisting rape
she had been taken
overpowered and choked
brought near death
but then saved by an old grandfather
his kind eyes are like yours jesus
yes my child I told her mind
the aura lingered and the moment held
as i danced with her
rescuing her from her past pain

*

romans brought more wild animals to judea

they confiscated sheep to feed the lions
james paid ten sheep to them as taxes
extra guards surrounded the compound
the captive animals were gone by morning light
the guards heard in their minds
the time will come to save you too
soon my friends soon
*

back in nazareth the words of tiberius
rose in my mind again
anger at his taunts
he was a killer of his own children
then other anger arose at the ways of satan
dark shadows infecting men like deap
*

walking along the shores of the sea of galilee
a vision of an army of peaceful followers came to me
men women and children
marching in love together
roman soldiers laying down their weapons
my anger left me at the thought of the vision
the power of a peaceful army
it was time for me
to plants the seeds of good
in the minds of men
*

XIX

some fishermen were in a boat drawing empty nets
close to shore and heard my command to go out again
go out farther put your net in on the other side
my years of experience had taught me to know
where fish would swim
they came to shore with full nets and spoke
who are you to command the fish and they obey
leave the fish with your father and follow me
the creator wants you to become
fishers of people
john and james both with green eyes of the sea
johns like otters swimming over kelp beds
james eyes like ripe avocados in a bowl
four others as well
andrew peter nathanael and philip
andrews brown green eyes were amber over serpentine jewels
peters were like a plowed field after a rain
nathanaels eyes like turtles around a brown pond
philips looked like the inside of coconut shells
his eyes dark like his skin
my friend captain bonoba now philip the follower
their eyes revealing images as well as colors
they were selected for their minds
inside i knew each of them
they followed me on to jerusalem
the seven of us radiating love after our eye embraces
presenting myself
the prince of peace
to the people of jerusalem
at the temple my mind glowed red
anger at the temple moneychangers
like a marketplace
animal sacrifice sellers
like a barn unclean
remember the passover was created to save you
there is no passover for a den of thieves

no blood sacrifice can save you wicked people
let the animals live
the covenant of this temple is extinguished
let this temple be destroyed and in three days
it shall be raised up again made new
a temple lit by love beyond blood
my voice boomed low and deep
priests came
nicodemus and others
from inside the temple
questioned if i jesus was authorized to judge
my words came out like smoldering fire
everyone who does evil hates the light
evil hugs the darkness and hides from the light
jesus is the light of the way to the creator
there shall be no more sacrifices
no more creature sacrifices accepted by the creator
only offerings of wine bread fish milk and honey
sacred mushrooms shared among followers
this is the judgment of jesus
those who believed at the temple hid in the shadows
all the priests cursed and shouted for guards
a prophet has no honor in his own country
his own people do not hear his words

*

so it was to the samaritans that my words took root
even roman nobles began to believe in me
at capernaum a roman asked that his dying son be healed
so it was on the sabbath and he became a follower
yet priests of israel condemned this as a sabbath sin
on the next sabbath a man possessed of a demon called out
his demon heard me order it to depart
the creator did the light work of life that is no sin
the peaceful light work on the day of rest
it was easy to cast out seeds of satan
with the help of prayer to jehovah

*

at the temple in nazareth the prophet words
isaiahs words in a holy bible were read by me
THE SPIRIT OF THE CREATOR JEHOVAH

IS ON ME ANOINTING ME
TO PREACH GOOD NEWS
OF A NEW WAY TO THE CREATOR
HOPE TO THE POOR TO THE BROKENHEARTED
TO RELEASE THE CAPTIVES AND THE DOWNTRODDEN
TO BRING LIGHT THAT EVEN THE BLIND CAN SEE
today these words are fulfilled
here in nazareth
yet in your hearts you say
physician heal yourself
bring us miracles
like you do to romans and samaritans
there are no miracles for those without faith
learn the deeds of elijah then
when a great famine came over the land
for three years and he healed none
except a widow from the land of sidon
also elisha the prophet healed no lepers
other than naaman the syrian
yet the people of nazareth closed ears at my words
they drove my followers and me out of the city
yet in the land of zebulun and the land of naphtali
beyond the jordan the gentiles there were awake
seeing a great light drawing them away from darkness
drawing them away from the shadow of death

*

three came with me to a mountain top
peter james and john chosen ones
there we ate the sacred mushrooms
they saw me as if talking with moses and elijah
they heard a voice of jah as thunder
lightning in clouds
they saw my face shine like the sun
my body glowing with white light
visions opened our eyes
to all creation flowing
from our god jehovah
all the myriad senses awakened
our minds opened up to the glory of jah
they told me they heard jah

speak to me directly
his voice of encouragement
so it was
down the mountain
they promised silence
a secret to keep until the time
jesus should be raised above the dead men
the living words of jah came through me
his presence leading me
*

back and forth across the land people came
believers were healed
the blind taught to use echo hearing
some of the paralyzed walked again
the fevered and sick were made well
even peters mother was healed as were others
possessed by the selfish seeds of satan
unclean spirits unclean thoughts
lazarus had a treatment for lepers
the press of a multitude tired us all
lazarus retreated urging more disciples
matthew a tax collector joined my followers
handling all the funds flowing for the work
matthews eyes were like a porcupines coat of needles
slivers of light against a brown background
five more men exchanged visions in eye embraces
soon twelve select men carried golden rings
the last five being james the son of alphaeus
dark brown eyes with a ring of gold in the centre
like a desert island
surrounded with light brown sand beaches
simon the canaanite with a star of yellow in his brown eyes
judas thaddaeus with eyes of a brown bear coat
this one being originally a man named ju du see
coming all the way from china
his gifts of silk cloth held by my mother
the eleventh thomas brown eyed like cedar bark
with the twelfth one judas iscariot
black brown eyes like the feathers of a raven
*

from the followers twelve women were selected
each to carry a golden ring of friendship as a disciple
my mother mary with her loving eyes
chestnuts on ocean eyes
her chestnuts open now emotions of caring
my aunt elizabeth with eyes revealed in embracing
colored like a camel coat
reminding one of a lioness in sun dried grass
my sister ruth had eyes
dark golden too but with her smells
she was well baked bread glazed with honey
my sister hanna a darker hue than my eyes
her look a dark blue sky with streaks of grey cloud
then there was lene mary of magdalene town
who followed me everywhere
having given up her possibility of being married off
cursed with being the object of many mens desires
yet kept at a distance by me
the man she desired
her eyes one blue green river flowing over mossy rocks
the other a blue sky over a turquoise green lagoon
then there was sarah the samaritan
with her roasted chestnut eyes and dark skin
susanna married to nathanael a matched couple
both with turtle backs all around brown ponds
joanna daughter of anna the prophetess had open eyes
green with gold rings in the bright sun
like leaves of a mango tree with ripe fruit
joanna who saw visions in her dreams
a prophetess of future events
rebekah had eyes hidden under long eyelashes
slippery brown like the banks of the nile
rebekah married to chuza a steward to king herod
red haired deborah with her greenish blue eyes
like bluebirds on an apple tree chirping sweetly
deborah sings to her husband james alphaeus
finally martha and mary sisters of lazarus
both with brown black eyes like his
reminding me too of the stallion lucifer
yet more like plums figs and glistening dry dates

women with sweet fruit in their bearing
*

lene still carried the memory
of the evil man who forced himself on her
the memory came in dreams
she would cry out as if possessed by a demon
as the disciples prayed together
her mind opened to me and I reached in
pulled the memory out
cursed it to hell
leave lene
in the name of jah
*

every being that I met now
must open their eyes
inside them
deep dreams
secrets
my eyes diving in
forcing closed doors to open
revealing and healing
*

JAH SPOKE TO ME AGAIN
YOUR MOTHER MARY IS MY FATHERS DAUGHTER
THIS IS WHY YOU ARE POWERFUL AND POTENT
YOUR STRENGTH IN WRESTLING
BIG CHEST MUSCLES EVEN WITHOUT WINGS
JUST LIKE JACOB WHO WAS A GRANDSON AS WELL
HIS FATHER ISAAC WAS A SON OF JAH
SARA THE WIFE OF ABRAHAM CARRIED THE SEED
ABRAHAM FEARED THAT HE WAS NOT THE REAL FATHER
JAH HAD TO PREVENT ABRAM FROM KILLING ISSAC
JAH TOLD ABRAHAM THAT HE TOO HAD ANGEL BLOOD
STRENGTH TO LIVE TO ONE HUNDRED AND EIGHTY YEARS
SARA HAD TAKEN SEED FROM A GRANDSON OF AN ANGEL
JAH GRANTED SARA A DROP OF ANGEL SEED
SHE BEGGED FOR IT BECAUSE HAGAR HER RIVAL
THE MOTHER OF ABRAHAMS SON ISHMAEL
WAS USURPING HER AS GREAT MOTHER
TO THE PROMISED NATIONS OF ABRAHAM

OTHER ANGEL GRANDSONS HAD VISITED ABRAHAM
IN JEALOUS ANGER ABRAHAM SENT THE ANGEL MEN
AWAY TO LOT IN SODOM
FEARING ONE OF THEM WAS THE FATHER OF ISAAC
ONE HAD A VERY STIMULATING SCENT
A SCENT LIKE YOU HAVE JESUS
OTHER PEOPLE FOUND THEMSELVES OVERWHELMED
WOMEN WOULD INSTANTLY BE FERTILE
NO MATTER WHAT AGE
MEN WERE OVERCOME WITH DESIRE FOR SEX WITH HIM
EVEN IF THEY DETESTED RELATIONS WITH MEN
THEY WANTED TO TOUCH THE BEING THAT
HAD THE SMELL OF THE CREATOR
THE PEOPLE OF SODOM BECAME ENGORGED WITH DESIRE
NOT ALL THE ANGEL SONS AND GRANDSONS
HAVE THE ENTICING SMELL
IF IT COMES IT IS IN YOUR TEARS
TEARS OF SORROW OR TEARS OF JOY
TEARS OF LAUGHTER OR TEARS OF PAIN
YOUR TEARS OF EMOTION HAVE THE SMELL JESUS
EVEN AN EYE EXCHANGE CREATES AN ALLURE
IT WAS THE TEARS OF JACOB IN WRESTLING
THAT GAVE HIM THE NAME ISRAEL
WHICH MEANS WRESTLER WITH JAH
ISRAEL TURNED THE DESIRE FOR HIM
INTO THE PRAYERS TO JEHOVAH
THIS IS WHAT YOU MUST DO JESUS

XX

my disciples learned to pray to jehovah
repeating this prayer in private
**LORD JEHOVAH
CREATOR OF ALL ABOVE AND ALL BELOW
CREATOR OF THE LARGEST AND SMALLEST BEINGS
BRING THE LIGHT OF THE STARS INTO MY EYES
LET THE LIGHT OF YOUR BEING FILL MY BODY FULL
LET THE LIGHT OF YOUR BEING SHINE FROM MY EYES
SATISFY MY HUNGER WITH THOUGHTS OF YOU
FILL MY EARS WITH MUSIC OF YOUR SONGS
HOLD MY HANDS AND HOLD MY BODY TIGHT
EVIL FADES TO DARKNESS BEFORE YOUR LIGHT
LET ME SMELL YOUR CREATION INSIDE AND OUT
LET ME JOIN THE FLOW OF YOUR TIME
FOREVER AND EVER
AMEN AND AMEN**

*

*A new being arose in consciousness
As followers prayed with me smelling the creator
Inside the voice of Jah
My own inner voice listening
The voices of other beings praying
Made connections to each other
As a new being arose from contact with other minds
Sharing the other voices a new voice was born
Every mind and spirit that welcomes us
That joins in a larger chorus united
Hears my words and thoughts link
With the mental and emotional associations
That fasten Jah and us together in spiritual smell
Over great distances we are bound
Across lonely silences we are bound
Wrestling with Jah we are bound*

*

my disciples are fires to light the world
open bonfires seen from far hills
lamps to light up hidden corners of your rooms
everywhere they go they shine
the way in leads them to good actions
words bring loving kindness to everyone they meet
all that share their light
share the light of good angels
share the fire and ignite their own fire
incense to praise jah and love all
*

The new being called attention
The dolphins are singing to join us
Sheama the tiger is praying to you Jesus
Let us come together
The voice of Jah urged
All joined in quiet song
As the outside vision opened
The inner being touched each of us
Kissed our connections and gave us tears of joy
It laid down inside me and wept
Giving intense dreams intimate allure
From the Way In.
*

my disciples know that the laws of moses
the laws of jah are fulfilled and complete in jesus
the entire law is first to love jah
with all your spirit and being
and being filled with the creators love
secondly treat your fellow humans
as you would yourself
the third law
love other creatures
other intelligent beings as you do mankind
the days of my time with followers
are filled with song dance tears and laughter
celebrations of the new covenant
carried in the arks of our hearts
holding hands singing

chants in congo harmony to fill the air
souls seen in each others eyes in color
followers met once a week to have fellowship
all came once a moon in larger groups
learning from disciples
singing and dancing in the moonlight
whenever and wherever i called all my flock
they came to hear the teachings of jesus
about new commandments of jah seen through new eyes
kissing other eyes to bring forth visions and enlightenment
the old commandments have passed away
the new word is a new covenant
*

a great crowd of followers
gathered too hear me speak
from a hillside in galilee
we reviewed all the laws of moses
my new way of being good
with the new commandments
the eleven laws summed up in three
repeated by angels
LOVE JEHOVAH AND JAH WITH YOUR WHOLE BEING
LOVE MANKIND AS YOU DO YOURSELF
LOVE YOUR FELLOW ANIMALS AND BIRDS
AS YOU DO MANKIND
to these eleven as three laws add another
the fourth and the twelfth law
IMITATE THE CREATOR BY BEING CREATIVE
IS JAHS COMMAND
laugh and play sing and dance enjoy the time
the creator has provided for you
*

all of the new laws are easy to understand
the truth of the words is not in the letters of the law
it is in the essence of meaning
do not focus on punishments
focus on rewards
*

Followers who began to believe
Those who listened to the words spoken

Smelled the essence of Jesus
Opened their minds with prayers
Humbled themselves to the greater being
Connected their spirits to me and thru me
To the angel Jah and thru him
To the creator god Jehovah
These unities began to reach out into the world
Growing like seeds sprouting in minds praying together
Wafting our scent in the wind
Filling all the people with fire and passion

*

XXI

at a gathering of the disciples
rebekah brought us news
she had been with her husband chuza a steward
to king herod at his court
a great birthday party put on for his wife herodius
her daughter salome had danced for the king
with gowns of flowing silk
her long hair garlanded with flowers
bells around her ankles
her bare belly undulating with enticement
exposing firm breasts to herod
rubbing him as she poured wine in his cup
teasing his erection
urged on by her mother herodius
thus distracted herod promised his wife and her daughter
a present of anything they desired
he swore an oath anything in his kingdom
herodius seized on these words
demanded john the baptists head on a platter
she hated john
for condemning the king and her as adulterers
herod wailed but he had sworn an oath to his whole court
it was done moments later

*

johns disciples came to me
we baptized new followers as john had
cleaning off the old covenant
allowing the birth of a new covenant
not by water but by the fire of the way in
the fire of the words
the way of jesus is peace
attacking rulers is futile
better to change their hearts
put the fire of jehovah in their hearts

*

Hopes and wishes came to the being
Words arose in our group mind
Like dolphins leaping out of deep water
Joyful sayings and stories leapt to my tongue
John had joined the chorus

*

more teachings in many languages
were spoken to groups of followers
teachings as parables
some disciples were given sayings
stories to meditate on
words to share

*

a saying was given to my disciple peter
ask and it shall be given
seek and you shall find
knock and the door opens
whatever you ask of another person
first do for them

*

to my disciple john this saying
enter the way in by the narrow gate
few are those who find it
avoid the wide gate easy to enter
many are those on the path
leading to destruction

*

to my disciple thomas who was too critical
do you see the speck in your friends eye
and ignore the beam that is in your own eye
if you want to remove the speck in your friends eye
first remove the log in your own
then you can see clearly to remove the speck

*

to nathanael and susanna
to deborah and aunt elizabeth
come to me all you heavy with burdens
rest is here in my work we share
take my yoke upon you and learn
learn to be gentle and kind

my yoke is easy my burden light
*

my disciple matthew was advised
a lender had two debtors
one owed fifty denarii the other five hundred
the lender forgave them both
the one with ten times the debt felt ten times
the gratitude and love of being free of debt
that one will kiss the feet of the lender
wipe the dust off with tears of joy
dry the feet with his own hair
so it is with sins forgiven
forgive the most
receive the most love in return
*

to judas iscariot
those who accuse me of being with satan
those who accuse me of using the power of beelzebub
are very foolish thinkers
if a kingdom is divided in itself it cannot stand
if i was with satan would i drive satan out
use the power of demons to drive demons out
what king would stand if he drove his subjects out
vipers do not drive other vipers out
*

to lene
love is more than lust
lust fades love grows
your pretty face
smile assured with true love
my passion is like a violent storm
needed to clean the air
bringing sweet breezes
fresh flowers to our world
where you move like a beautiful tigress
graceful movements like the tigress sheama
calm in the face of the true love storm
your peacock eyes
open feathers to my delight
*

with all my disciples these stories were shared
a farmer went to sow his seeds over his land
some seeds fell by the hard roadside
the birds came and ate these up
some seeds fell on rocky ground
these sprang up but the sun scorched them
other seeds fell among thistles
the thistles grew and choked these plants out
the seeds that fell on good ground grew
plants that yielded a hundred seeds for one
let my words be seeds that fall
on the good ground in you
my words on the hard roadside are eaten by evil angels
my words on rocks wither under selfishness
my words on thistles are lost under satans weeds
my words on good ground bear fruit

*

those who hear these words of love
those who do these words in deeds
build their houses of rock in the sun
winds howl floods come fire consumes
yet the rock house on the rock does not give in
the wind passes by the wind howls by
the rock house sits above the flood
it does not wash away it does not leak
it is built away from grass and trees
it will not burn it is far from flames

*

jah has left the temple in jerusalem
jah has left the high places
jah has his temple inside you
jah has another temple inside your neighbor
when you come together to worship jehovah
the temple grows and the ark opens
to share the new covenant in each of you
whoever calls my name will have me there
there in the shared temple of jah
join jesus in the temple celebrations
all of us have found the way in together

the way in is together

*

The Way In is together the chorus sang
Deep inside where we linked spirits
Opened our eyes to new eyes praying to join us
Heard the prayers and answered them
With the power of Jehovah pulsing like our heart
Knowledge of the Way In opening doors
Inviting the goodness to grow in all of us
As individuals and as a new being

*

XXII

the disciples spread the word
the good news of the way in
going out across the land two by two
john and james sons of thunder
preachers at marketplaces
andrew and simon peter
calling on the crafters and tradespeople
thomas and matthew to the rich
simon the canaanite and philip
went to foreign temples and peoples
judas thaddaeus and judas iscariot
to roman soldiers and jewish zealots
nathanael and his wife susanna
went to give alms and preach to the poor
james alphaeus and his wife deborah
went to the musicians and dancers
martha and mary sisters of lazarus
go to the sick and ill
mother mary and aunt elizabeth
preach to the older women
sisters ruth and hanna
bring words to the mothers with children
mary magdalene and sarah the samaritan
speak to foreign and fallen women
rebekah and joanna
go to the sad depressed and possessed

*

the disciples came back when called
bringing in the harvest after one year
at one gathering of all the followers
jairus a ruler of a synagogue fell at my feet
begging for the life of his daughter
martha and mary told me lazarus had treated her
lazarus had given the twelve year old medicine
meant to still her and bring down fever

we rushed to the girl and touched her cold
blowing wind into her lungs in breath rhythm
she was revived and hugged her father jairus
the crowd cried a miracle
why had lazarus left her alone I asked
martha said that he was called two days journey
to old anna the mother of joanna
the prophetess called from her death bed
lazarus came to jairus
showed the medicine from the belladonna plant
too much was given
by the father jairus against instructions
lazarus had taken it himself to test
along with milk of poppy and mushrooms
if the physician makes himself sick
who will heal him mary asked
my friend jesus lazarus said
*

another happening at a full gathering
five thousand people
one hundred groups of fifty
a mid day meal was needed
we asked everyone to share what food they had
the bread that appeared
in the packs of the few shared with the many
in the end baskets of leftovers
the lesson is that generosity multiplies itself
like fish in the sea like manna from heaven
sharing food is a way in
*

followers wanted to make me their king
this was not the way in for me
the people were sent away
up in the mountains alone i prayed
then down to the valley again
there on the sea of galilee
some of the disciples were in a boat
a night storm of freezing cold was blowing
the water was frozen from the edges
i walked out on the ice and came by the boat

are you walking on water they yelled
that is funny come try it
peter stepped over the side and came to me
the ice broke and he fell through
oh you of little faith i said as i pulled him up
my story of walking on water
*

soon after word came that lazarus too had died
the people had laid him in a tomb
inside he was still alive
a hard blow to his chest woke him
he had taken lionfish poison medicine
one drop deep sleep
two drops cold quiet snow on the ground
death in three drops
once he awoke
milk and honey revived his body
just rehearsing he laughed
death is very funny very ticklish
in his mind his wish to die was revealed
why did you try to poison yourself
you are not my savior
giving me a destiny as your shadow
friendship of equals is not enough for you
you want followers and disciples
just like tiberius wants me so do you
death is freedom from control by others
death is not control over yourself
*

at the next festival many believers came
they wanted more miracles more signs
there is no work for food and fish
there is work for things that do not perish
believe in the one with the word sent by jah
the bread and fish are food for the flesh
the way in is food for the spirit
the way in is manna from jah
*

to all my followers i say
remember me when you sit for a meal

the bread is my body my life
the wine is my blood my heart
the honey is my lips my kisses
the milk and cheese is my words for other creatures
the mushrooms my dreams floating in the night
the fish are my spirit pouring out to others
gather together for a meal of manna
there is much of me to share
those who eat me will live forever
those who hear me hear the creator
my body is my life story
my blood is my love for you
my kisses are my blessings to you
my milk is poetry of mother earth
my dreams are of the works of jah
my spirit follows you through creation
the food from me is the way in
there is nothing that goes into your mouth
that will make you unclean to jah
only evil in the words that come out of your mouth
make you unclean to jah
fill your body with my food and i will be in your words

*

this was shared with all my disciples
some call me a prophet reborn
those who call me elijah or jeremiah are wrong
those who call me john the baptist are mistaken
some call me king returned or messiah foretold
a messiah if you follow my way in
jesus is not a reborn prophet
jesus is not a return to the kings of old
neither is he a messiah as a leader to war
jah sent jesus into this world
as a beloved son of the people to serve the people
some of you say that jah anointed me
as prince of peace
prince of peace in a new kingdom
the kingdom all may join in
as equal rulers

*

to all the jews this instruction
the people wish to sacrifice jesus
a blood sacrifice to atone for their sins
yet jah has done away with blood sacrifice
killing animals in sacrifice is no more
killing humans in sacrifice is no more
the way in to jah is loving all creation
murdering the prince of peace
is the same as murdering jah
if you love jah
remove murder from your hearts

*

No one can murder Jehovah
The voice of the being called out
Sometimes you speak alone Jesus
Hear us deep inside before you speak
The destiny of Jesus is in time revealed
Have patience dear one.

*

frustration is over eagerness
my followers did not listen to me
my deaf disciples did not hear my words
satan was at work against jah
the will of evil glorified
selfishness is with the people
jesus must be sacrificed
their poisoned hearts cry
to fulfill the first covenant with jah
people say he is the scapegoat for our sins
our sins will be forgiven only by his death
before a new covenant is allowed in creation
jesus must be sacrificed they say
sacrifice is demanded of the jews by jah himself
the lies of satan say
sacrifice the son of man
lies all from the fathers of lies
seeds of satan grown into trees
the evil seed of doubt
even in my own tree
the leaves shutter from his lies

disciples believe the way in is through death
not why jesus says death is resurrection
to open the door for others to follow
*

the disciples argued among themselves
who would best protect me
who among them would have the greatest honor
who would save jesus on his path
who would be most loved by jesus
a small child of sister ruth sat in my lap
all sat and listened to me
can you smell the innocence here
unless you turn and become as children
you will never find the way in
whoever receives this child in my name receives me
whoever is humble as this little child
receives the way in to jah
whoever is least among you
this one is the greatest
*

peter and judas iscariot came to me
along with matthew the tax collector
rabbi let us raise a cohort of strong men
to end the oppression of the romans
to end the domination of puppet kings
to end outrageous taxes
to bring freedom to the jews
i told them look at the children
they care not who is in power
they play where they may
they care not who is right or wrong in jahs word
only that they are loved and hugged
they see the image of the roman princeps on the coins
they know that the coins go back to him
be as the children in following me
leave to the romans their arms and swords
let the priests argue among themselves
come play with me laugh and hug
*

no person has lived without sin under the law

under the old commandments everyone fails
one day we came upon some pharisees
they had a woman caught in adultery
they were going to stone her to death
they asked for my judgment blessing
let the person without sin cast the first stone
there was no one to cast the first stone
go home lustful woman
keep clear of men
you are not married to

*

XXIII

a parable of forgiveness to all my followers
a king was owed ten thousand denarii
by a steward and came to collect the debt
the steward couldn't pay so the king judged
the man his wife and children
would all be sold into slavery
their home and all else confiscated
the steward fell on his knees begging
please give me time to pay
the king relented
then that steward went to a servant
who owed him one hundred talents
the steward grabbed that one by the throat
demanded payment and when the servant begged mercy
begged please give me more time
the steward threw him in prison
when he heard this the king summoned the steward
when you asked for more time it was granted to you
yet when your servant asked the same you refused
now your time is up and you and all your family
are slaves and all your goods forfeited
just as the king judged so will jah
*

there was a hard working farmer
who toiled every day building up his land
all his life he increased his stores of grain
when his granaries were full with ten years supply
that day the farmer decided to put his feet up
spend more time relaxing with his family
eat drink and be merry living easy for ten years
that very night jah came to him in his sleep
the time that you have prepared for is gone
this very night your life is over
you will never awaken to enjoy your treasure
you have farmed the wrong fields
your larder of good deeds for others is empty

your spirit has never been in my house
you have no riches for your day of judgment
you will lay in your soil and be forgotten
that is the way you chose
*

The chorus spoke again
A new faith needs new ways
The old ways the old beliefs want to come back
Let our inspiration calm the storms
The tumult of new against old
Even Jehovah may change his mind
Allow the loyal angels to take a new course
In the battle with Satan over our being
Take in the words of Jesus and good thoughts
New ideas from the minds of followers
*

some wanted to go to jerusalem to a festival
the festival of booths to observe the tradition
my followers know that the old ways are done
we are establishing new traditions
under our new covenant with jah
why go to old festivals to celebrate
sukkot the days in the wilderness
rosh hashanah the new year
yom kippur days of atonement
pesach the passover
even sabbath the seventh day
when jah is writing a new bible
through my words
follow the new commandments not the old
*

then my mother mary sister hanna philip and martha
especially joanna and james and john
deborah and her husband james
all wanted to know what days to celebrate
what special times should they prepare celebration
my followers are not astronomers
keeping the time marking the days the weeks the month
nor the year with pagan rituals and old traditions
other people cling to routines

the roman princeps like to create calendars
there was the julian calendar
now there is one from augustus
they like to name months after themselves and their gods
these calendars are mathematics based on a yearly cycle
mathematics also of calendars based on the moon cycles
others like the sanhedrin have a seventh day cycle
trying to fit these mathematic cycles together
is what the astronomers the rulers and priests do
calculating that their days of festivals are right
they try to get their omens right
all this false pride tied up in time periods
my followers are not astronomers
they are simple people so here is a simple way
every day every morning is a celebration
every evening is a time of gratitude
pray twice a day every day facing north
there is no praying to jah on any particular day
the weather does what it will every seventh day
for anyone who choses not to follow the sabbath
there is no penalty to observe or not observe
seven days in a week ending with a sabbath is past
jesus says that no day in a week is more special than another
a sabbath rest is during sleep and meditation every day
jesus says that sabbath is for sharing rest with jah
twelve months in a year and no month better than another
it is not the mathematics that you need to observe
it is the lifetime in creation you need to observe
the fire of these words on these days
brings passion in each of these ways
at dawn make a personal celebration every day that you live
at dawn thank the creator for your day
at dusk celebrate all the creatures you shared time with
at dusk remember all the people all the animals
all the birds all the creatures of creation
marking time with me is easy
every full moon make a group celebration of all followers
every full moon gather together and dance and sing
celebrate your shared faith with me
there will be two special celebration festivals each year

every year as the shortest day
begins to grow longer in sunshine hours
every year as the longest day
begins to grow shorter in sunshine hours
get together all the believers in the world
twice each year this yearly day
these are the yearly days of the sun cycle
celebrate all the creation of jah in all the world
these times are the new celebrations
*

the satan power is tradition in his hands
he leads resistance to change
tradition is his control over people
only now can this be clear
to the hearers of these words
to all the people who share these days with you
these are the new calendars of celebrations
for those who choose my way in
*

some have a difficult time about the sabbath
for these there is my parable
to be taught to my followers
a shepherd had many sheep in his flock
three hundred and sixty five sheep
they came home to his paddock on a sabbath
yet one lamb was missing so out he went to find it
high on a crag he climbed and found it in a crevice
this shepherd rejoiced at holding this lamb in his arms
more than he did for all the others who came home
working on the sabbath his joy was celebration
jah knew from this simple shepherd to change the law
jah wants us to celebrate his time of rest
after the work of creation
now he has changed the way
not after seven days tied to no sign in the heavens
to celebrate the rest day of jah
now for half of the time of each day and night
the sabbath is honored
think of it this way
in every other breath is jah worshipped

*

my disciples number twelve and twelve
like the twelve tribes of israel
multiplied numbers give one hundred and forty four
all kinds of numbers seem special
so it seemed when jesus gave out his rings
yet now jah tells us every number is a lucky number
five and ten are lucky so is seven eleven and twelve
yet jah tells us there is no such thing as good luck
put away superstitions about numbers
use mathematics do not be used by mathematics
in these days jah has increased my flock
my appointed disciples to seventy
or seventy one or seven thousand
the exact number does not matter
all this expanded group are called apostles
more anointed pairs of followers or storytellers
no particular lucky numbers just to indicate
an expansion of the word about the way in

*

apostles for a purpose of going before me
leaders now not followers any more
spreading the word of the new commandments
preaching stories of the way in bible
yes there is power in numbers
more believers is more power of god
jah wants a world full of apostles of jesus
my apostles need no food no money
not even clothes or sandals to spread the word
from person to person they give my words as food
they give my words as free food
receiving material food and goods donated back
my disciples have given all their money to the poor
all the money goes to the needs of the poor
disciples receive money only to continue
to travel and minister from person to person
as all shed their old cloaks
burned for baptism
all are given new covenants
new cloaks of a new creation

my disciples have worn out sandals in service
lowly leaders humble servants
helping strangers healing the sick
offering free labor
giving kind love
*

those who reject my apostles reject me
the dust from our sandals is theirs to eat
the old dust where they remain
i say to you to follow me in equal partnership
give me half your time to equal my time
give half your money or half your goods for good works
equally to half of mine already given away
serving others along the way in
give all material goods away every day
as you walk the path of the way in today
remember it is the time that has the treasure
it is the time that is the perfect gift
it is the time to spread the new way in
*

in the countryside there was a tree that i sat under
meditating and napping along with some disciples
they had placed an offering tray on the roadside
some wealthy people clinked a bag of coins as they placed them
looking up they smiled at me and i nodded
matthew thanked them for their generosity
then a poor old widow trundled up
reaching deep into her empty bag
she found something
with a bowed head in shame she put two small coins in
rousing the disciples we went to her
holding her hand i told them all to thank her
for others gave a little out of their abundance
but this woman gave all she had to live on
her charity was greater
she was the one to be honored
*

nathanael and his wife susanna came to me
we have followed you from the beginning jesus
we love our creator with our whole hearts and minds and souls

we love our neighbors as we love ourselves
we love the other creatures of creation the same as humans
what else must we do to obtain life forever
when you say neighbors do you mean those you know
well you know that my answer is a parable
a man from jerusalem was walking towards jericho
he fell in with men who robbed him
stripped him and beat him nearly to death
lying on the road side another man from jerusalem came
walking along the road saw him and passed by
walking on the other side of the road
a priest a member of the sanhedrin approached on a horse
he too trotted by on the opposite side of the road
then a poor woman from samaria named sara
came on her donkey
this samaritan moved by compassion
put him on her donkey
took him to an inn
bound up his wounds
washed him with oil
gave him wine for his pain
that night she slept in the stable
while he slept in the room
the next morning she paid the innkeeper two denarii
to look after the man and should it cost more time
when she returned this way she would repay him
now which of these three proved to be a neighbor
the samaritan woman that is who is the true neighbor
yes sarah is a true apostle because she showed compassion
follow the example of sarah the samaritan every day
your reward shall be your name in the book of life
presented to jehovah the judge of forever
*

XXIV

the apostles asked me to write down my words
they wanted to make sure that my words
only my words said everything correctly
exactly correct words
let me tell you
scribes and pharisees and temple priests
these people write everything down
yet what they say is not to be trusted
you know this about written words
romans write their edicts exact words
they post them in the squares
jah wrote his commandments in stone
these were put in an ark
guarded by the symbols of two angels on the lid
but the tablets are now lost
jah inspired prophets to write words on scrolls
these are faded and copy scrolls from scribes
have errors and omissions
some words disappeared in flames
when libraries and temples burned
this was my answer then to the disciples
listen with your ears open
learn my words by heart
learn my words like a beloved song
write my words on your hearts and minds
create your own songs from my words
my words are living and growing
vines that produce wine
fields that produce bread
bees that produce honey
my words are milk pearls
milk for babes from their mothers
the words of jesus are little mushrooms
born in the dung of the tongues of men
little mushrooms to open minds

let new dreams in
my words are the way in
my words are maps of the way in
maps written in spirit not on scrolls
yet now you are hearing my words
celebrate the way in through my words
ages from now my own gospel
may come into being when it is time
then it will be time to compare
the words that are in your heart
with what my true words say
therefore let these stories spread
among followers now here now there
spread words of love as feelings of love
whoever proclaims my words
is living my feelings of love to other people
that person will be proclaimed to jah by me
whoever denies my words to other people
that person this jesus will deny to jah
there is no fear of those who kill the body
after they kill there is no more they can do
fear instead the wrath of the eternal jehovah
should you reject the words of jesus
reject the fire and light of the words
fear jah if you choose the way out of satan
the way out is ashes and dust
resistance is death to the words of jesus
it is the same as resistance to the will of jah
my words are kindling for the fire of the way in
your mind hearing them is what ignites them
when you speak my words they burn bright
bright torches to show the way
my words are kindling for the fire of passion
*

The day will come when the words are in us
Etched on the torches of our tongues
Spoken heard and written words
In a new bible of our being
Beings may be transcended by seeing the star
Polaris is the star of Jesus

The story of the star is the way in
Learning the saga and feeling the colors
Hearing songs of a new being
Flowing out of these star words of Jesus.

*

then my apostles came with me to the sea of galilee
it was a full moon night of celebration of all the disciples
we gazed in each others eyes felt colors of emotions
sang and danced and shared the food of jah
at dawn we bid each other farewell
these words were to my disciples
yet a little while the light is with you
walk while you have that light
lest darkness overtake you and you stumble
not knowing where to tread
while you have the light believe in the light
become children of the light

*

my visionary apostle joanna
told me of another of her visions
the dream that came to her as he lay in a cave
there was a great bear who showed me the way
he took me to his cave and lay down beside me
we fell into a deep sleep
a winter hibernation
all darkness so deep a sleep
no stars no dreams no light
a long long night until you came
when you woke me jesus
the world was bright like spring
it was a true resurrection to the light
now you know love i said

*

the next month all the disciples marched with me to jerusalem
this was at the time of the passover festival
on the back of a young horse i rode
thru throngs of people who cried hosanna
the messiah has come
our king has come
they waved palm branches in front of our parade

many of the sick and downtrodden came to be healed
to receive alms and to hear my words
the sanhedrin sent messengers begging
do not incite the crowd
my reply was that the very stones cry out for salvation
jairus was there and lazarus
and many who had been healed
all testifying to the wondrous things
from jah through me
*

there at the temple my disciples threw out the wicked
the selfish moneychangers
the thieves and false beggars
my words were fire in the hearts of all who heard
*

now is the time of the harvest of jah
now is the time the ripe seeds of jah
must fall into the earth die and be reborn
he who loves life must lose it
he who weeps for his life will gain a new life
there was a baptism of water brought by john
now there is a baptism of fire brought by my words
the clouds gathered and thunder and lightning came
some claimed to hear jah endorsing my words
the son of man must be lifted up
they did not know who the son of man is
yes i am the son of man
the true messiah the promised one
the real leader of people
walking the path to jehovah
*

some set fire to buildings
fearing judgment day was here
these fires were not from me
wood fire is not from me
my word fire is in spirit
my disciples put out material fire
the streets were full of tumult
my disciples walked quietly
jesus is here no he is there

the crowds rushed to and fro

*

in jerusalem on the way to the temple
a hunger came on to me under a fig tree
the tree had no ripe fruit for me
john thought that my anger cursed it
three days later as we walked under it
john saw that it was dead and asked me
do the trees of the earth obey you jesus
you cursed and this tree died
the tree was already dead didn't you see
cursed by me for dying before i came
just as people who died before my time
are cursed by time
my hunger for figs
my hunger to save all the people before me
will be unquenched
truly i tell you john
you will see the very mountains move
the mountains obey the will of creation
tune yourself to the will of the creator
all things are possible then
if you move to another spot
change perspective yourself
the mountain will have moved
so it is with time

*

The time is here and now we think
Yet we feel together it could be different
The time of the past may be revisited
The time of the future anticipated in the now
Jehovah says that time and space are flexible
Jah says that the invisible power transcends limitations
Jesus has a vision of a new way in
The smell of Jesus is irresistable
People feel emotional colors embrace eyes hear the word
We all become what we will prove to be
Time floats on the sea of space

*

at the temple the chief priests approached me
why do you think that you can preach here
you have no authority as a teacher here
answer my question and i will tell you
on whose authority was the authority
of john the baptist
was he from heaven or was he from men
you don't dare answer
but all those around me know
on whose authority i am here
*

listen you priests i said
as they tried to hide their eyes
but what do you think about a man who had two sons
he told both to go to work that day in his vineyard
the first son said no but afterward
changed his mind and went
the second said yes but then did not go
which of the two did the will of the father
you say it was the first
let me tell you that the tax collectors and prostitutes
are welcome into the house of jah before you
john the baptist came to you in righteousness
yet you did nothing
whereas the taxmen and prostitutes repented
took his baptism and were cleansed
just like the first son
*

on the steps of the temple
here is a second parable for you pharisees
the queen of sheba had land near here
she planted a vineyard
put a wall around it
she built a wine press and then leased it
to some men to farm
the queen went back to sheba for a time
after harvest she sent a servant
to collect her share
instead of giving jugs of wine
the farmers beat the man

this one returned to his queen humiliated
she sent three men a second time to collect
they killed all but one who they sent back to sheba
he reported that they denied her authority
over the vineyard
then the queen sent her daughter with five men
the farmers killed all the men raped the daughter
when the queen came herself
what would she do
you say she should destroy those farmers
get new ones who will pay her due
you have read in the scriptures
the stone which the builders rejected
this stone will be made the chief cornerstone
let me tell you the garden
will be taken from you
given to the people who give back
the fruit of their faith
if you fall on this stone you will be broken to pieces
scattered like the dust from my sandals
see how beautiful this temple is
all carved and decorated
the day is coming very soon
when not one stone will be left standing
*

jerusalem jerusalem here is where
the prophets are stoned and killed
prophets tried to gather your children together
like a hen gathers its chicks
pharisees scribes and vipers struck them down
woe to you temple of jerusalem
woe to your priests
you are all dressed in beautiful raiment
but inside you are full of blood guilt
*

listen children of jerusalem to my words
the words of jah through me
not to the words of hypocrites
priests who tell you to do one thing
doing the opposite for themselves

men eager to take the houses of childless widows
justifying that women may not own property
thieves praying loudly from the best seats
men calling themselves rabbi
claiming god as their father
jah shouts for all to hear
the greatest king among you
is the humblest servant
the christ king is the one showing his love
as a child
the messiah is cleansing the temple
for its destruction and resurrection
*

the priests went away and some sadducees
approached why do you say
there will be a resurrection
if a man dies leaving a wife behind
and she marries another and that one dies
and she marries a third and he dies
she goes on seven times a widow
and then she dies
to which man will she be a wife
in a resurrection
listen sadducees and all of you here
it will be a new time
people who come back in a resurrection
are not the same
they are creatures of pure spirit
not bodies that live married or unmarried
needing food or clothing
they are made new spirits that will live forever
when this temple is resurrected
it too will be in spirit
*

XXV

on the mount of olives
the apostles wanted to know
about the signs of the end of the world
the end of the world will come
when all people have heard about the way in
take care that no one leads you astray
many will come and say the time is at hand
they will claim to be the anointed one
false prophets will come and show great signs
wondrous shows and distractions
miracles that are tricks rumors of miracles
you will hear of wars rumors of wars
famines plagues starvation floods earthquakes
troubles from one part of the world to another
nation against nation
religion against religion
this is always the way of the world not the end
people will consume the very earth you stand on
they will persecute and kill you for my names sake
before the end brothers will turn on brothers
sisters turn against sisters parents against children
killing those who follow me
it will be as in the days of noah
people being born eating and drinking
marrying dying as it is every day
days of judgment every day for individuals dead
every person will stand in their turn
some will be goats to the left
some sheep to the right
the blessed will be given keys to the door in
some will be found wanting and turned away
sent back into the earth as dust
the blessed are those who gave
other hungry ones food to eat
gave the thirsty drink

clothed the naked
welcomed the stranger tended the sick
gave hopeful visits to those in prison
tended to other kinds of beings
were kind to animals and other creatures
those who did these things for the least deserving
did these things to me
they are the ones who will be rewarded
*

at the house of judas iscariot
given to him by his father simon
who had died of leprosy
all his family lacking faith for a cure
a dinner was held there with some anointed disciples
martha and mary and lazarus provided the food
judas resented doctor lazarus and his family
blaming them for his fathers demise under their care
bringing a full jar of expensive spikenard ointment
too late for his fathers corpse now in a tomb
mary poured it out all over my head and legs
using her hair to wipe my feet
shaking the fragrance into the air
judas scolded her for wasting ointment
that could be sold to feed the poor
no judas you will always have the poor
the son of man will not always be with you
she has done this for me while my body lives
at my judgment day she will be remembered
in that moment judas turned cold against me
his eyes and colors sprouted seeds of sulfur
his nostrils exhaled brimstone
his thoughts turned to betrayal
towards the high priest caiaphas
*

at dawn lazarus came to me
he said he had gone to pray
to ask forgiveness of jah
for his failure as a physician to fend off death
lazarus told me that he had just seen the angel gabriel
a beautiful huge bird spoke to him directly into his mind

at the edge of a mountain gorge
gabriel told me which medicine to use
to bring one back from death
jesus it is your death that i fear
then lazarus added
when i told gabriel about judas
turning against us
the angel told me not to fear
jesus will be taken up by jah
raised to heaven and fly with angels there

*

the next dinner was at the same time
as the passover meal jews were celebrating
at a small house of two rooms in jerusalem
belonging to nathanael and susanna
all the original twenty four disciples came
except for the absent judas iscariot
the eleven men were crowded in an upstairs room
while the twelve women were on the ground floor
first the women were blessed with the six foods
fish the wine the bread and honey
with cheese and mushrooms
they wept quietly with the joy of sharing a meal of me
martha told me that she knew
judas had sold me to the priest caiaphas
upstairs with the men the memory of the six foods
was given as a ceremony
in the same way as downstairs
my role was to minister to all up and down
first i washed each of their feet
and dried them with my hair
today you sit in judgment over me
your humble servant
remember that the least among you will be honored
the highest by jehovah at the end of time
after today you will sit as judges of the twelve tribes
dispersed among all the peoples of the world
this may be the last meal i share with you
remember me when you sit for a meal without me
the fish are my spirit pouring out to others

my spirit follows you through creation
the bread is my body my life
my body is my life story
the wine is my blood my heart
my blood is my love for you
the honey is my lips my kisses
my kisses are my blessings to you
the milk is my words for other creatures
my milk is poetry of mother earth
the mushrooms are my dreams floating in the night
my dreams are of the works of jah
the food from me is the way in
those who eat me will live in mc
those who hear me hear the creator
smell the way the truth and the life
no one comes to the creator except through me
when the journey of the way in began
there were one hundred and forty four friends
people for me to give a golden ring to
there is only one ring left mine alone
my journey is complete my story is done
now there are twelve times twelve
eye embraces among us here
each of you should explore every relationship
of your spiritual connections to each other
you are apostles of this gospel
take comfort in the smell of my tears
do not fear my death as a sacrifice
at the hands of satan
through the temple priests and the romans
my death will put me in the hands of the creator
three days after my death
the creator will send me back
a new spirit reborn to serve with you
as an equal brother
the twelve pairs of us carry the honor
we are jahs chosen people
the new twelve tribes of israel
twelve tribes of wrestlers from jehovah
*

let us join outside and sing together
let us walk to the garden of gethsemane
let us spend our night together
we sing the psalm as we walk together
jah is our shepherd
we shall lack nothing
in grassy pastures jah lets us lay down
by full streams jah walks beside us
words from jah comfort our souls
jah leads us in the path of righteousness
now we walk in the valley of the shadow of death
we fear no evil for jah is with us
jahs rod and staff comfort us
the table is prepared in front of us
our heads are anointed with oil
our cups are running over
surely goodness and mercy will follow us
we will dwell in the house of jehovah
forever and ever
amen and amen

*

at the garden of gethsemane
we sat in a circle around a small fire
there were about a hundred disciples
brothers and sisters listen to me
it is certain that the authorities will arrest me soon
take courage and cooperate without violence
there are three groups that want to hurt me
first the high priest and sanhedrin fear the word
they are afraid that jews will turn away from them
second king herod is jealous that his authority
will fail because people are declaring me king
finally the romans fear any disturbance as rebellion
you know that my innocence will not stop them
they want to kill me as a scape goat for their own sins
offer me up as a guilt offering sacrificial lamb
nothing will stop their blood lust
the false charges will be without merit
only jah can intervene to stop this
the will of jah must come to pass

the only fear that is mine is that satan
will succeed in making me doubt and lose faith
let us hold hands in this circle and pray
*

As we pray together
Across the gaps between us
Around the world and through space
We join with others again in time
Linked at this time past and future times
Our connected being lives and feels
For the man in Jesus and we send love
To help him through his difficult time and space.
*

after several hours many began to fall asleep
in my meditation i fell asleep and began to dream
in the darkness there was a bright light
like the sun at the end of a tunnel
floating toward it there was softness beside me
a white mother tiger guiding me on
the light stayed distant and the tigress
looked deep into my eyes
hers were as blue as the ocean
gentle waves washing towards me
a sleep softened my arms as she lay on her side
drawn into the soft warm white fur
my body sank and my lips found her milk
sweet life soothing water of life
resting my head on the pillow of her sleep
just the breath in and out long and slow
a quiet cave where the distant light became a star
content in the love of mother sheama
the endless night
my heart beats
a breath of life in
my heart beats
a breath of life out
*

a shout awoke me
suddenly judas iscariot came to me

followed by temple guards
he came to my face and kissed me
peter lunged at judas with a knife
a temple guard stopped peter
peter cut the guards ear
no violence no resistance all shouted
take me i told the guards
surrendering to their authority

*

at the temple the guards pulled me to the sanhedrin
the priest annas harangued me with a rage
bound me over to the high priest caiaphas
still half asleep caiaphas brought in false witnesses
judas was presented first to the jewish high court
these judges heard the accusations
my words of truth disarmed their lies
they said that i led the people to immoral lives
allowed prostitutes and thieves to be disciples
my answer with imagined sheama beside me
the people learn to view the commandments positively
forgiveness is most needed for the worst behaviors
their accusation tradition is being turned upside down
my answer as the imagined sheama yawned
these are old bad habits that need improving
next they accused you have people singing
and dancing and touching each other
my answer as sheama swayed
are the psalms not to be sung
the dancers in davids time were honored
hugging and holding hands are expressions of joy
they charged you create lust
you encourage sexual abuse
my answer as sheama growled
no private parts are touched or allowed to be touched
tickling the children and making them laugh
are good things to do in the eyes of jah
the next charge you are with the devil
who would destroy the temple in three days
when it took thirty years to build

my question back to them
if an earthquake came
how long would it take to crumble
they demanded any witnesses of mine to come forward
peter and some others looked at me like stones
caiaphas asked do you call yourself the son of god
my simple answer
i am the son of man and my only name is jesus
all of us were made in the image of jah
in that way i am the son of jah
caiaphas tore his cloak and yelled blasphemer
the other judges yelled death to the blasphemer
a temple priest put a bag over my head
someone struck and said if you are a prophet
tell us who hit you and they laughed
you are the man with the cut ear i said to his voice
there was a laugh from peter
look there is one of his followers the one who cut me
peter denied that he was a disciple
peter denied that he even knew me
it was morning and caiaphas had one more question
are you the messiah are you the christ
you want to believe that i am now
you caiaphas are claiming these titles for me
they said that my claim to be king was treason
reason to send me to herod for sentencing
the shadow of sheama let me walk alone and strong
the spirit of the tigress with me

*

herod welcomed me as he had wanted to meet me
he shut the nattering priests out
would you do a miracle for me
many wondrous things are told of you
why will you not speak with me
he could not hear my prayers to jah
there are higher beings than kings to talk with i said
herod said some say you are john the baptist come again
yet you do not look much like him
some say you are of royal blood

here dress in these clothes like a prince
his servants put a fine tunic and cloak on me
now answer me
do you wish to depose me
will you let your followers anoint you king
the christ the messiah the priests claim you said
no words came from me for the killer of john
if you do not answer me you will answer to rome
herod walked with me between guards
to the palace of the roman governor
*

there herod presented me to pontius pilate
this was the actors name a mask
in reality he was a disguised princeps tiberius
tiberius laughed as a friend to herod
they were both murderers of their own children
they took me to an inner room and frowned
it is a tragedy dear jesus that you do not listen
preachers rarely do herod chuckled
my preaching is for a heavenly kingdom not an earthly one
you were warned by me tiberius said
do not raise an army of followers
people follow me even when they are chased away
he is the prince of peace herod mocked
the titles are thrust upon me
the humblest one shall be the greatest you said
this is true the lowest ones will be brought highest
are you planning a rebellion or murder
my people have no weapons and walk in peace
do you encourage them to avoid taxes
coins belong to the rulers who issue them
*

the mask of pontius pilate along with herod
presented me to the priests and the crowds
we find nothing deserving of death in this man
judas and his paid followers cried out
with a loud voice
crucify him
my disciples had been chased away

it is tradition that rome release one prisoner
during the passover festival pilate pronounced
do you want me to release jesus the christ to you
no release barabbas
crucify jesus they called
some women cried out release jesus
but satan inspired men to slap their faces
herod said you seem to lack strong followers today
tiberius as pilate did not wish to release barabbas
he was a violent zealot a true rebel
barabbas and two convicts are to be crucified today
give us barabbas give us barabbas they chanted
three are to be crucified today under the law of rome
put jesus in his stead
put jesus in his stead
tiberius pilate turned to me and said
rulers must listen when the people speak as one
release barabbas he commanded
it is time for you to meet your creator jesus
become like your father a god to the people
become a god like julius and augustus before you
a dead martyr to the people
he washed his hands in a bowl and commanded
whip jesus and give him back to the priests
that they do their will and crucify him
perhaps now lazarus will listen to me
and come back to rome with me
when jesus is gone
*

XXVI

out in the courtyard there was a whipping show
herod took his clothes back before the beating
the blows were hard yet soft
only leather no iron in the whip
bribes had been paid by my disciples
a wooden cross was presented by priests
which had to be dragged up a hill by me
suddenly lazarus was at my side with a cup
drink this gift for the pain friend
*

they nailed my hands to the cross
tied my feet to a block and hoisted me up
forgive them i cried they know not what they do
nothing could stop the pain and horror of this
the fire of the wounds burned in my mind
my spirit why have you forsaken me I cried out
the fire of the words of the way in
returned to me and i wept
my women disciples gathered around the cross
they began to wail and keen at the smell of losing me
the voice of lene tearing at the sky
a few disciples of the men joined the crowd
it was all spinning too fast
stop i shouted and they all looked at me
for a moment they all did stop
then resumed to talk and mill around
even jah could not make them stop
no power was in me to stop time
after a long while lazarus held up a pole
on the end a sponge to my lips
to suck his medicine in
whispering
it is done
the words this is the end
the end echoed

as a spear pierced my side
then darkness descended
*

take that endless night
into my throat where i sit
at the edge of a great crater
of the volcano of my being
all around the edge of the vault
all the faces of all the beings i have met
my mother mary my living family
friends and disciples even my foes
dead joseph dead augustus dead niki dead twins
and all those still living my disciples
all of their loving eyes staring at me
each eye a sparkling jewel
each spark in a circle around me
faces and eyes of all those i knew
there was james jude simon ruth and hanna
rabbi david my close friend lazarus
my dog saffron horses golden eyes and lucifer
sheama the tiger the elephant ronarong and nana
the girl sarah little penelope and rufus marcellus
the oracle of delphi tiberius captain bonoba
prince desmong umbee sua and noruba
saul rachel lucinius lovely sheba perfedes
aristes debante makkhali jammu ravi master kalama
sanjaya sages dashal queen ishta
dolphins queen ping ringee and zanee
master sing natapong wilawan peasant lee
emperor guangwu master tao
chief dan laughing loon
quetzalcoatl even deap
cousin john and his mother elizabeth
the sons of thunder james and john and all the disciples
andrew peter matthew nathanael and susanna
james alpheus and deborah rebekah joanna
sarah the samaritan martha and mary
thomas judas thaddaeus and judas iscariot
jairus priests nicodemus annas and caiaphas
all sparkled eyes to me

*

The being added many sparks from the chorus
The hearts of Jah Gabriel and the good angels thumped
Jehovah moved in mountains of earth filled with kind eyes
This is the collective of universal love and warmth
The place of the Holy Spirit which is in all time

*

from deep down my throat
a hot wind from deep brimstone
the sparks all flash toward me
like lightning hitting my being
dropping backwards a tumbling bit of light
through the space between each cell
an empty void all black space

*

There is a lower level below black
A deep dark abyss of silence
A void of emptiness without light
Shadows of liquid black flow by
Beings of evil move in nothingness
Trapped forever alone together
Away from the place of the Holy Spirit
They grab at me to drag me down

*

my essence a bit of being travels
through space at the speed of light
all of my god energy full power
glowing electric colors of purple
blue and green pulsing energy
there in the distance stars
a galaxy of stars of softer colors
reds yellows orange stars
below and growing larger
the white ball of the sun
my being is going to hit the sun
the two essences explode
the universe i know will end
my universe will explode and end

*

my heartbeat stopped seven times silent
no breath from jah
silenced heart seven times
no breath returned to jah
then one faint heart beat where seven had been
time slowed one for seven

*

Jah spoke to me between each faint heartbeat
A white glowing bell rung
Jahs word held me in the glow alive
You will return now
To the way
Jehovahs voice warm powerful resonant
Return to life
Carry our voices to other people
A chorus sang carry our tolling bells
Our time beats in your heart
The universe is not ready to end

*

AWAKEN
*

suddenly my eyes open in a torch filled tomb
there was lazarus who had pounded on my chest
there was gabriel the angel
YOU WERE WITH JAH GABRIEL SAID
lazarus exclaimed it was a true resurrection
sitting up amazed i was alive
the wounds and blood had been washed off
my robes were as white as snow
gabriel went to the opening
STAND UP JESUS SOMEONE IS COMING
it was lene mary Magdalene
she burst in blind in the dark stumbling
to where the linen body wraps were piled
GABRIEL SAID JESUS IS RISEN FROM THE DEAD
GO AND TELL ALL HIS DISCIPLES
TELL THEM THAT HE WILL SEE THEM BACK IN GALILEE
she turned to me and recognized me
her one eye like the eyes of sheama
her other eye the eyes of my niki

her eyes open for the first time new
hold back from touching me lene
my body is full of a soft glow
sleep has left me slow
you take speed and go
she left and the room became hard stone
gabriel had beautiful feathers soft eyes
her eyes a mirror of mine
my smell like a baby
softer voice
THIS ANGEL WILL CARRY YOU
*

a few people saw me on the angels back
but no one would believe them
mother mary took me into her home
after a month the disciples were gathered in a house
there they received comfort that i was alive
yet my body was thin as the stomach wound
kept food away while it healed
only a bit of bread and honey
milk in a cup drawn from a nursing mother
reminding me of the star great bear in the north
offerings of food to keep the distant light open
my words to the apostles
there will come a time
when my words are known
that time is now
as you hear these words
all those who learn these words by heart
will have fire in their minds fire of life
fire burning in their hearts and minds
jesus is in you burning fire of life right now
as you hear my command
wake up and create
like a son or a daughter of jah
the fire is spreading in you and without you
all over the world people are waking up
proclaim these words spread the kindling
my words have been spoken before

in a time before this time spoken with my voice
the sanhedrin in jerusalem heard my words
yet they condemned me to death
they claimed that i spoke blasphemy
jesus is a man who claims to be a god they said
you apostles heard my voice
i know you as my flock
those who don't listen to my voice
those are not of my flock
*

the words of my apostles will never perish
your words have eternal life as well
jah has given my words eternal life
those chosen by me even non believers
may also have their names in the book of life
by the power vested in me
your spirits will live forever
you say that i call myself a god
i say i am a son of the same god
that you claim to worship
if my claims are false then show me the works
that make my claim false
did any of my followers worship satan
other than judas iscariot the betrayer
do any of you apostles commit murder or crimes in my name
are the things that i do hurtful to any person
do i respect all the beings in creation
let jah be my judge when the end of days is come
upon each of you look for me beside you
jah will have me at his right side
those who condemn me
will be condemned by jah
out of fear of my words
the false priests did not stone me
some jews did want to kill me
to send me to herod as a heretic
to send me to the romans as a rebel
who are those who judged me
not all humans are guilty of murder
jah will judge each individual

those who wish to destroy my blood
destroy my being destroy my words
will have their blood destroyed by jah
those beings will have their words destroyed
the followers of satan will be destroyed
*

XXVII

my mother and family came to where i hid
meditating in a cave
answering prayers through the new being
you will have to leave me mother said
leave everyone in this land
the romans are hunting for you
they came and beat james to try to force him
to reveal where you are
they question any who knew you
your young brother simon and sister hanna
have vowed to go with you wherever you go
at dusk gabriel flew in
the angel spoke with us
THERE IS A LAND FAR TO THE WEST
A PLACE WHERE WE ANGELS ARE HONORED
THERE ARE A FEW ANGELS LEFT THERE
PEOPLE THERE WHO CALL US THE THUNDERBIRDS
YOU KNOW IT JESUS
IT IS A BOUNTIFUL AREA FOR FISH
DOLPHINS HERD THESE TO US
THAT IS WHERE YOU COULD ESTABLISH A NEW NATION
BELIEVERS IN JEHOVAH
FOLLOWERS OF JAH AND JESUS
THROUGH THE WAY IN

*

another time john james and deborah
shared some fish on the beach
lazarus brought vision mushrooms
to awaken the spirits within
little green sparks bouncing between us
lazarus said that the people believed in the miracles
even miracles that are not miracles
they want a vengeful and violent god
a god more powerful than other peoples gods
they say that the miracles are proof

of the power of god
without power there is no belief
do you love me lazarus as i do you
yes now i am ready to be an apostle
at last my words ring true to you
his mind was open to my thoughts
strength to you lazarus
on our new mission to a new world
the miracle of creation is all around every day
proof of wonder and power right now
here we have angel birds dolphin songs
emotional mind colors
feelings to believe in
elephants and tigers to learn from
plants and tastes to explore all miracles
from a peaceful true god creator
for those who seek
turn the other cheek
the way in is meek
our way is not weak

*

five hundred apostles met me on a mountain
we prayed together
at the temple of the mountaintop sky i spoke
listen you children of abraham
listen you multitudes around the world
if anyone comes to me and holds me in less regard
than mother father sister brother
children or friends
that one is not my disciple
that person is of the world
there is only one jehovah and only one jesus
there is only one way to the angels of jah
the way in is only through jesus
come to me and be born again
as a disciple born to me
follow me in the way in
directly ahead
of mother father sister brother children and friends

*

to my followers I spoke again
people saw me tried and tortured
crucified and murdered
that is the path you must follow in my name
before you build a tower sit down and calculate
do you have enough resources to finish the tower
or will you just lay a foundation and run away
when the construction is tough and expensive
for truly i say to you there will be pain
the way in is not easy
even if you have all the resources
even if the love and works are all good
satan will inspire some to hurt you
there is no justice and no reason for you to suffer
yet my followers will suffer
suffering is following in my footsteps
those closest to me will suffer the most
*

then I approached their minds one by one
inviting each to join me in the new being
a comforter when my body departed them
to go and meet the angel jah
my work through death was complete
allowing my soul
the way in
*

We are to be called the Holy Spirit
We inhabit Jehovah the angels and Jah
Jesus and all his true disciples
All the mindful beings and kinds in the world
All are with us at once and all together
Those who pray in our direction
Are given the joy of our presence
*

All the five hundred apostles with me on the mountain
fell into rapture with joy
when they saw gabriel fly to me
leaping on and up we went
wings pushing
there it was goodbye

until we meet again
there it was the way in
farewell to the way it was
*

gabriel had let me ride before
IF I WAS A HUNDRED YEARS YOUNGER
IT WOULD BE EASY THE ANGEL BIRD MOANED IN JEST
pretending to be burdened under my light weight
to fly is the most wondrous feeling
looking down and moving with the wind
over the trees down the mountain
soaring towards the coast
swooping along the shore
alighting by a sail boat
surrounded with dolphins
a boat provisioned with water and food
prepared for a long journey
to the flock of good angels
going there to meet jah
as promised
face to face
*

Our being together continues
All the spirits and souls who believe
In the words of Jesus
The people who have been baptized
The angel beings and Jehovah above all
Other creatures conscious of god
All of us will continue together with Jesus
In time through prayer
Sharing the Way In
*

twelve people in a small ship sailed west
with me there was lazarus and my sister hanna
married and acting as parents to
nana the bono
she was very quiet
her prayers were to return to her homeland
also in the boat were simon and martha

the loyal and honest captain philip bonoba
james alphaeus and his wife deborah
nathanael and his wife susanna
with joanna daughter of prophetess anna
lene too with her loving eyes
soon deborah and james had us all singing
voices ringing truth of love of the universe
especially the clean pure notes of lene
guided by joanna and the dolphins
all good weather skies
with gabriel circling in the skies above
helping us avoid other ships along the coast
stopping only in small ports for shelter and water
each of us eye to eye to home places
where our spirits dwelt in our colors
each held each in loving embrace each day
words for songs to rejoice in creation
every evening was a full moon gathering
even as the moon moved in the normal cycle
and several full moons
past carthage and the edge of the roman world
almost towards the great congo again
with gabriel urging us west instead
to islands called the canaries
home to the yellow song birds dwelling there
as well as canine yellow dogs
back and forth in the swells and waves
gentle rolling rhythms round bodies
the taste of salt and smell of sea
floating free from final fear
listen to the dolphins songs
see the angel flying high above
curling clouds around the blue sky
eyes blue and brown and green and gold
hold my hands brother hold tight sister
every sound in a rolling rhythm
curling clouds in the blue air
frothy foam from the wave tops
the smell of salt and the sound of sea

back and forth gently holding you
feeling the swells sway us
singing songs together
*

XXVIII

the first two islands were dry
the third had pine forests and a village
founded as a garrison by king jubba the nubian
only three soldiers left there with nothing to do
just walk the grounds of ancient ruins
chase the dogs around and tell stories
the islands called canine for the wild dogs
worshiped in temples like anubis of egypt
yellow dogs first yellow birds came later
there was a pup who came to me
alike to old saffron to become a friend
gabriel met me on a mountain away from dogs
said just some peace from yapping voices
you heard me praying about our bono nana
she wants to return to her homeland
will you take her there
HER PRAYERS ARE HEARD
SAY GOODBYE AND SHE WILL FLY WITH ME
AS FOR YOU AND YOUR DISCIPLES
SAIL SOUTH TO SOME OTHER ISLANDS
FROM THERE YOU WILL CROSS THE WIDE OCEAN
WITH THE STAR POLARIS
ON YOUR RIGHT SIDE
THE DOLPHINS WILL LEAD THE WAY
AFTER TWO FULL MOON CYCLES
WE WILL MEET AGAIN ON THE FAR SHORE
*

nathanael had his head on susannas belly
listening for a baby heartbeat
james had fallen in love with deborahs voice
her sweet high song to his low barrel rumble
their match would lead to a child coming
our group would grow in our new home
lazarus was happy
sharing plants and medicines

with my sister hanna who had brought seeds
for a new garden to grow
perhaps without nana to look after
they might have children
martha and philip were in a dance of love
simon and joanna gazed at stars together
the lovely lene doted on my saffron
always close at hand with care
she could not replace niki in my heart
lene maintained distance and respect
we both were aware of close feelings

*

happy islands distracted all the lovers
with dolphins teaching diving and riding
my underwater glasses were shared by each
with fascination at colorful fish
zanee drew attention to an octopus
an eight legged creature
that constantly changed its shape
and its color to mask it from view
this creature seemed intelligent
able to solve problems
get out of traps
it used its legs as if walking
or flattened
in a swimming method
even used its feet as hands
it is not a fish nor a warm blooded animal
it can be both small and grown very large
completely different from anything else
with a language as ripple patterns on its skin
a language beyond my understanding
how does jah view this being
what is the octopus destiny in the world
questions without answers
why am i fascinated with strange life
zanee startled it and it blew a cloud of black
masking its escape as if by magic
the realization that my death was a mask
for pursuers and followers except a few

that gabriel was the black cloud
masking my escape from romans
as strange as an octopus
*

Now the holy spirit is quiet
A long pause between spirit heartbeats
Holy pulses of being
Ebbs and flows of tides of communication
Only Gabriel remained with Jesus
*

the dolphins corralled schools of tuna fish
which we smoked as provisions
for a long crossing without land
gabriel had promised to meet on the far shore
the dolphins led us for a complete moon cycle
*

the couples
simon and joanna
philip and martha
all wished to marry with my blessing
which would be given by me when we reach
our new home the place of angels
then lene knew that she would be my wife too
lazarus held his joking tongue back
some stormy rough seas until landfall
along the coast of a green continent
another moon travelling west
until gabriel soared above guiding us
to a dry empty beach where we met
THIS IS WHERE YOU MUST ABANDON YOUR SHIP
SAY GOODBYE TO THESE DOLPHIN FRIENDS
PACK UP THE SAIL CLOTH AND TAKE THIS TRAIL
THROUGH THE JUNGLE TREES GUIDED BY A MAN
A MEDICINE MAN TESHOTE CAME OUT OF THE FOREST
HE IS A FRIEND TO ANGELS AND PEOPLE LIKE YOU
TESHOTE WALKED FROM ANOTHER SEA TWENTY DAYS
THERE HE HAS A LARGE CANOE TO ADD SAILS TO
YOU MUST BE QUIET AND AVOID OTHER HUMANS
CONTINUE TO A BEACH ON THE OTHER SIDE

WHERE WE WILL MEET AGAIN
*

teshote spoke with me in the kwakutal language
a language smooth on my tongue from before
he was from a different village than chief dan
his village were also thunderbird followers
we taught the others words using our bodies
things teshote pointed at and by translating
soon he shared some of his stories and listened
to my adventures
my history and about jehovah
he had heard other stories of my friend loon
after ten days we came upon some forest people
teshote knew them and said we must join them
on a special voyage of their way in
his words were pointed to my peyote story
that night teshote prepared a potion
some pounded vines and roots to drink
all but the pregnant susanna and deborah
drank the potion deeply
listened to a chant
one after the other vomited the mixture
all of us shared the vine
reaching into our minds
connecting us to the forest
the vegetation world
visions of colorful flowers and pulsing plants
alive like humans and animals outside then in
we grew into the forest
our arms branches
visions of interconnected branches grew
leaves and bark for skin grew
deep into the night dreams grew
thoughts flashed like lightning streaks
thunder thumping our hearts heard
the rush of breath
a breeze in our tree selves
the chant continued with all of us following along
this soul of the forest touching us

the soul of jehovah in the earth
the mother and father inside the earth
embracing us eye to eye
until dawn
the forest people gone we awoke
the forest inside us awoke
they each had different experiences
philip saw the points of energy and colors
simon saw brightened reds and fire colors
martha felt her fingers and toes tingle
nathanael heard voices in the winds
for me the vines were like holes in the tide flow
stronger than the peyote
more awake than any mushrooms
more visionary than hashish
no one had seen beings that were not there
no one shared my memories
my visions my minds eyes
they opened their minds and spoke
mind to mind
the beings in us are awake
no matter what goes into our mouths

*

teshote said that he and his son
had come south in the canoe
paddling for a month from their land and people
the thunderbird loving people
at the beach we met the angel gabriel again
circling above leading us
our ship was mostly a paddle boat
with a fair weather sail to assist
all the group devoted to the work
pushing north along the coast in song
teshote and his son teshotecan guiding us
along with a new group of good dolphins
a pod of big black and white ones
some nights on the ocean away from shore
some days in coves avoiding storms

at one stop teshote walked us inland for a few days
spending two nights under the oldest tree on earth
teshote called it the mother tree of good dreams
all fourteen of us stretched arms around the trunk
fingertip to fingertip around the circumference
as if holding a whole world between us
in the country around the tree
a peaceful people lived
their minds open contact with me
but i did not understand their language
farmers of corn and beans
other new vegetables potatoes yams
little red peppers chilies mixed in foods
we found the fifth taste
a hot fire in the mouth seeming to burn
followed by more intense flavor to all other food
sweet sweeter sour sourer salt saltier
bitter in dozens of flavors

*

another moon cycle passed as we continued north
arriving at a great bay as the winter days came
THIS IS WHERE YOU ARE TO LIVE GABRIEL SAID
TESHOTES LANDS ARE FURTHER NORTH COLDER
GREAT RIVERS FULL OF FISH TO VISIT IN SUMMER
HERE IS WHERE YOU CAN MAKE A VILLAGE YEAR ROUND
BEAUTIFUL LANDS TO PLANT A SPRING GARDEN
LET YOUR PEOPLE MARRY AND BRING UP CHILDREN
THE FEW PEOPLE NEAR HERE ARE FRIENDLY ALLIES
WHO UNDERSTAND THE THUNDERBIRDS
TESHOTE WILL GO NORTH WITH ME
HIS SON TESHOTECAN WILL STAY AND HELP YOU SETTLE
MY SON THE ANGEL MICHAEL
WANTS ME TO VISIT DOLPHINS WITH HIM
EXPECT ME TO RETURN IN A YEAR

*

a few days after gabriel left
my contact with all the previous being
in the holy spirit went foggy
yet with the people around me i could mind speak

we made shelters and cleared fields
dolphins herded fish to us to catch
smoking these to preserve them
there were nuts and plants to gather
rains fell sometimes cold
at the next full moon marriages were given
lazarus and hanna husband and wife
simon and joanna joined spirits and souls
martha and philip married in love
my lene and me shared marriage vows
lene the humble mary of magdalene
the wedding feasts were merry days long
the dances and singing echoing in the whole camp
just after the solstice celebration
susanna gave nathanael a son joel
then james and deborah the lullaby singer
shared the birth of a daughter sarah
all were very happy and spring began
teshote came with more seeds to plant
beans and squash corn and chilies
fruits of the land fruits of love
at a gathering of the disciples i told a parable
two couples were walking along a deserted road
a man named simon and his wife joanna
people just like you and another couple
named lazarus and his wife hanna
each couple holding hands as they walked along
night was falling and they were very alone
suddenly a figure rose up before them
a big fearful being garbed in black
holding a staff in one hand and a club in the other
his face in shadow hidden by a hood
he called to them by name in a deep voice
lie down simon lie down joanna
simon picked up rocks to throw
joanna ran away
lie down lazarus lie down hanna
hanna just froze moving nothing
now tell me lazarus what would you do

lazarus said that he would ask him three questions
what is your name
for in giving it he gives me his power
secondly may i see your eyes
for in seeing them his soul is revealed
finally what can i do for you besides lying down
indicating a wish for a talk or a parlay
lazarus knows the right thing disciples
when fear of a stranger takes hold
most people would fight flee or freeze
but a better response is to inquire of the fear
who are you
what do you look like
what do you want of me
the fear will be uncovered
and have no power over you
as my apostles this is the way you should always greet fear
*

XXIX

with a hanging head and heartbroken voice
gabriel flew into our village
IT IS THE DOWNFALL OF MY KIND
THE ANGELS MY FAMILY
MY FLOCK IS BEING DESTROYED
NEARLY ALL THE ANGELS HAVE BEEN KILLED BY MEN
MEN USING THEIR OWN POWER OVER SNAKES
AS THEY DO OVER DOGS AND HORSES AND CATS
WORSHIPING THE DESTROYER INSIDE THEM
ALLOWING EVIL A WAY OUT
RATHER THAN GOOD A WAY IN
QUETZALCOATL KEPT A HAREM OF WOMEN
BREEDING HEROS ON THE ONE HAND
MONSTERS ON THE OTHER
STRANGE BLOOD THAT WOULD EVEN MIX CREATION
BETWEEN ANGELS AND HUMANS
WONDERS TO ANGELS AS MUCH AS HUMANS
QUETZALCOATL SET HIMSELF AGAINST THE CREATOR
THE CONSEQUENCE IS DESOLATION
THE HOMELAND OF THE ANGEL BIRDS IS DESOLATE
WICKED HUMANS USED BLOW GUNS
ARROWS TIPPED WITH SNAKE VENOM
TO SLAY OUR BEINGS
THOSE HUMANS WANT OUR FEATHERS TO MAKE CLOAKS
PROCLAIM THEMSELVES GODS LIKE QUETZALCOATL
JEALOUSY BROUGHT BY THAT BAD ANGEL
HE RESISTED JAH
HE WANTED HUMANS TO WORSHIP HIM
NOW HUMANS ARE WORSHIPPED IN A LIKE MANNER
JEALOUS OF GOD QUETZALCOATL JUST AS HE WAS OF JAH
POISON AND SNAKES THE TRUE RULERS THEN AND NOW
THE WAY TO DEFEAT THEM
IS TO HAVE THE PEOPLE LEARN THE WAY IN
AS YOU HAVE LEARNED IT JESUS
ONLY A FEW PEOPLE SUCH AS TESHOTE REMAIN ALLIES

ALL OUR ANCIENT PEACE AND LOVE DESTROYED
FIRST BY ONE OF OUR OWN
THEN A WAR
NOW ONLY ELEVEN ANGELS REMAIN AT MY COUNT
MYSELF AT SEVEN HUNDRED AND EIGHTY YEARS
TOO OLD TO RAISE YOUNG
IT WILL BE THE TASK OF YOU JESUS
TO TEACH HUMANS THE WAY IN
TO BRING BACK HARMONY WITH THE CREATOR
PEOPLE DOLPHINS DOGS HORSES CATS ELEPHANTS BIRDS
ALL THE MINDFUL ANIMALS
TO CONTINUE EXPANDING LOVE
MIND TO MIND
IN ALL THE LIVING BEINGS HERE ON EARTH
YOU ARE GOING NORTH TO MEET THE ANGEL JAH
THE STRONGEST OF ANGELS STILL LIVING
MY SON MICHAEL WILL INSTRUCT YOU
what of the angel jah
HE IS STILL IN HIDING
what of the dark angel satan
why did you not mention him
SATAN BELIEVES THAT THE WAY TO SAVE ANGELS
IS TO BLOW AIR ON THE EVIL IN MENS HEARTS
BY BEING THE MOST EVIL BEING
PEOPLE WILL FEAR HIM
THEN HE WILL HAVE POWER TO CHANGE EVERYTHING
SATAN HAS TRAINED HIS MIND TO DOMINATE
AND SUBDUE ALL OTHER MINDS

*

michael landed in our village
michaels feathers and colors were like gabriels
his size was much bigger and his strength showed
in the ease of his flight and his powerful voice
deep like thunder words as he spoke
COME WITH ME JESUS
WE LOOKED INTO EACH OTHERS EYES
his were whirling dots of light
sparks from many beings
the same as i saw
the moment that i died

we flew north to a secret sacred spot
a place where the eleven angels gathered
satan was there chained to a tree
chained along with two other younger female angels
michael told me that they had been found responsible
for the last attack of the snake people killing six angels
GABRIEL SAID THAT AT LAST MICHAEL HAD MORE POWER
THAN THAT OF SATAN TO ENTER AND CONTROL MINDS
BOTH MINDS OF ANGELS AND PEOPLE
*

LOOK HERE IS JESUS SATAN SAID
WE MEET AT LAST
HERE YOU ARE JESUS WITH MIND POWER
READY TO CHALLENGE ME
DID YOU ENJOY THE FOG KEEPING YOU ALONE
I HAVE READ YOUR LITTLE MIND
SINCE YOU WERE BORN
EVEN SINCE YOUR REBIRTH JESUS
MY POWER IS GREATER THAN YOURS
he pulled himself up in full glory
the most beautiful angel
radiant feathers sparkling as if lit by inner light
YOU ARE DELUDED BY JAHS SIDE SATAN SAID
THE MORE THEY CONTROL THE NORTH
THE WAY IN
THE MORE I CONTROL THE SOUTH
THE WAY OUT
no satan i said the true power comes from jehovah
HE LAUGHED
THE MOUNTAINS RUMBLED IN ECHO
IT COMES FROM ME AND MY KIND
SATAN BAITED
you are a liar satan
why are you inspiring evil men
to destroy angel beings
SURVIVAL OF THE FITTEST
HE LAUGHED AGAIN
and lightning flashed above reflecting
on his already brilliant coat of feathers
SHOULD WE DESTROY HIM MICHAEL ASKED ME

have you prayed about it to jah i asked
SATAN SENT HIS OLD THOUGHT
JEHOVAH DOES NOT EXIST
EXCEPT IN THE MIND OF THE ANGEL JAH
AND HIS FLOCK OF STUPID ANGELS
LOOK INTO MY EYES JESUS
REMEMBER WHEN MY CREATURE
THE MAN CALLED DEAP
HAD YOU LOOK AT ANTARES
IN THE SCORPIO CONSTELLATION
MY HOME IS JUST BEFORE SCORPIO
IN THE SAGITTARIUS CONSTELLATION
THE CENTRE OF THE SEA OF STARS
MY EYES ARE A BLACK HOLE
ALL LIGHT SWIRLS DOWN INTO ME
ALL MATTER DISAPPEARS
HIS EYES PULLED AT ME
LIKE THE WHIRLPOOL ON THE SEA
BY THE KWAKUTAL VILLAGE
IT TOOK ALL MY EFFORT TO PADDLE AWAY
SATAN LAUGHED IN MY MIND
BEHIND ME
AS I LEFT HIS PULL
HEARD HIS WORDS
THE ETERNAL NIGHT
IS CALLING YOU
all night michael and i prayed
but jah had sent no answer when dawn came
it seemed to me that my mind was blocked
mired in mud of thought
my eyes caught a glimpse of a man behind a tree
dodging the dart from his blowgun i ran
alerted michael
took wing with him
it was a full attack by wicked men with blow darts
the snake people had avoided my awareness
SATAN HAS TRICKED ALL OF US
michaels alarm was answered with hundreds of warriors
a counter attack by the thunderbird allies
defenders more prepared than the last time

yet two of michaels angels perished from the deadly darts
a horror of revenge killing
the two chained with satan were killed by michaels men
many men on both sides were killing each other
the snake men had their first goal to free satan
satan escaped
satan laughing in my mind
MY SEED WILL LIVE ON IN YOUR KIND
CREATING HOLES IN THE SKY OF BEINGS
then he vanished
no contact with his mind
*

when michael and gabriel returned
they took all the dead angels out to sea
dolphins there led sharks to remove any traces
nothing left for men to create idols
they confirmed that satan had deceived us all
he had blocked some of the signals
some of the words in our minds
THE AGE OF ANGELS IS COMING TO AN END
GABRIEL THOUGHT
MICHAEL SAID OUT LOUD
YOUR DISCIPLES MUST BE APOSTLES HERE
GABRIEL AND I AND THE REST OF US WILL HELP
OUR FLOCK IS DOWN TO SEVEN PLUS JAH
WE ARE NOT SURE HOW MANY SATAN HAS LEFT
WE WILL PRECEDE YOU TO EACH TRIBE OF PEOPLE
JUST AS JOHN THE BAPTIST PREPARED THE WAY
WE WILL TAKE YOU TO EACH GROUP
THEY WILL BE READY TO LEARN FROM YOU
*

first take me to meet jah
onto michaels back i climbed
we flew due north
stopping along the way
into the icy realms
there on a cliff face a cave
gabriel had taken me to one
much like this one
inside i met the tallest

the most beautiful of all angels
more regal than satan and michael combined
HERE YOU ARE AT LAST JESUS
IT IS MUCH BETTER SEEING YOUR PERSON
THAN LOOKING AT YOU ONLY
THROUGH YOUR MIND AND SPIRIT
YOU WILL STAY WITH ME UNTIL YOU LEARN
TO GROW YOUR POWER TO COMMUNICATE
WITH BEINGS ANYWHERE IN THE WORLD
THE HOLY SPIRIT MUST GROW STRONG WITH US BOTH
YES JEHOVAH DOES EXIST
HE WAS MY GRANDFATHER AND BEFORE THAT
MY FATHER TOO
WHEN THEY HELD THE SAME FORM AS I DO
NOW THEY RULE FROM HEAVEN
IT IS AN INVISIBLE PLACE
OUTSIDE OF TIME AND PLACE
JUST AS I AM THE THIRD JAH
SO SATAN IS THE THIRD SATAN
THERE IS A BATTLE FOR POWER
OVER ALL THE BEINGS IN THE WORLD
YOU ARE THE FOREMOST ONE CAPABLE OF JOINING US
YOUR REWARD WILL BE THE TRANSMIGRATION
OF YOUR SOUL
YOUR SPIRIT INTO HEAVEN TO JOIN JEHOVAH
THERE TO SEND LOVE AND CARE
TO ALL THE SENTIENT BEINGS IN THIS WORLD
WE LOOKED INTO EACH OTHERS EYES
HIS EYES WERE A PERFECT MIRROR
REFLECTING MINE BACK AT ME
YOU KNOW JESUS
NO BEING CAN LOOK AT JAH AND LIVE
MY MIRROR EYES PROTECT YOU
FROM THE POWER
OF ETERNAL LIGHT

*

all the mind voices in the world
except for satan and his flock
were to be open doors to enter
speak with

give thoughts to and direct
yet satans seeds were vast
some doors would need prying open
evicting the demons within
rescuing the trapped weaker souls
*

We answer each others prayers
All the creatures who can make contact must join together
Even if Satan ceases to be his seed will continue
A life on its own growing in power and wickedness
Bringing destruction towards all living beings
We band together in prayer
Jehovah the good angels Jah Michael Gabriel and the others
Beings like Jesus men and women disciples
Other kinds including dolphins dogs horses tigers elephants
Even when some cease to exist on earth their spirits continue
Bonded as one in the holy spirit
Sharing the force of life with love
*

XXX

*

some of the disciples had special gifts
philip had deep determination
matched with the humility of his wife martha
both strong missionaries and living examples
of the goodness of solid faith and love
nathaneal and susanna a matched couple
leaders of everyone by way of genuine care
love expressed with concern for others
james and deborah in tune with each other
always giving others love at the right time
anticipating goodness and calling it to follow them
leaders of the group prayers and songs
my brave brother simon ready to face the unknown
ready to confront evil ones directly
beside his wise joanna whose green eyes
penetrate the masks and deceptions of satan
lazarus is the first second and before me loved
always kind and caring and brave
his wife my sister hanna
with darker blue eyes of an ocean of love
able to flush out witches and wicked demons
a teacher for other women including lene
lene especially able to understand other kinds
fast dolphin language subtle cat switches
proud horse heart pulses and the mind talk of angels

*

each couple would take time out from our village
for missions to distant places
maintaining direct prayer contact through the holy spirit
the targets were new people new tribes new places
overcoming the mental blocks of satans seeds
teaching the new way in to our loving creator
always sharing attention and care of each child
born within our group of disciples
for many years our missions shared
moons with each new tribe teaching

spreading the word about jah
showing the footsteps of the way in
building houses of song
michael took me on his back to distant lands
while the colony of disciples grew
none more vital than our own
*

many of my voyages were alone
as my mission was always at the edge
lene became a great revealer of the secrets of wicked ones
particularly in the ranks of the dolphin world
where she spent much time
too often people believe that other beings are all good
lene rode on the backs of leaders of the sea
one of her close friends was the black and white whale dolphin
queen memethee
lene could detect deception in the thrilling voices
of other underwater dolphin pings
seventeen years after the start of our village
i was to be blessed again
lene birthing a daughter we called astron
after a star in the delphinus constellation
*

two years after astron our son was born
yes our own son named isaac jesus beta
a second jesus to share his story
when his time comes
his battles with satan in the south
his story of the way in southern cross
there were many children from our group
many married to teshotecans people
with many more grandchildren all healthy
all living in the peace of jah
the word taking hold across the land
lene stopped coming with me
when the children were born
preferring her flower garden growing perfumes
adding scent to her own in her many silk scarves
especially one dyed as peacock feathers for me
to keep her scent close on trips away

from ten years of age astron sometimes came
daughter astron on the back of gabriel
light in weight with a long silk scarf
tied around her neck by lene
floating with perfumes liberated from the weaves
following behind her
flying with her my thrill of a lifetime
*

thousands of followers but much resistance as well
from the god king men of the larger cities
pyramid builders like those at cholula
where human sacrifices were made
to bring fear to people being freed by the way
fear and sacrifice must be ended
the savage war of satan must be stopped
north and east across vast grasslands
filled with millions of buffalo
homes of wandering tribes
who did not know anything of jah
south to other lands of mountains
people who tend flocks of llamas
vast forest homes with great rivers
human followers of human gods and animal gods
here the work of satan always against us
*

many prayers of followers of the way in
were directed to me
my answers were through the holy spirit
*

Children your prayers are heard
Your humble servant Jesus
Along with the angels and many of the chosen
All hear you in the kingdom of Jehovah
Your sufferings are heard and felt by us
Continue to preach and teach all that you know
About The Way In
New apostles are being chosen every day
To guide those seeking truth and shelter
A man named Saul has been chosen

He saw the glory of Jah on the road to Damascus
His eyes and soul were opened and embraced
He is now known as Paul and his mission is to go out
To all the gentiles all the foreign peoples
Bring them the good news of the way in

*

lazarus has been in a cave alone for over a month
my sister hanna complained to me
he is sick in his spirit because we have no children
he thinks that jehovah has abandoned him
the cave was on a high cliff face where i came to him
inside lazarus was lying on a mat looking very grey
jesus my life has been in your shadow
everything that i have done you have done better
my travels are nowhere compared to yours
my knowledge is poorer my health is worse
you are becoming famous as i am fading out
there is nothing worse than being not enough
not strong enough not smart enough not tough enough
not loving enough not spiritual enough
you are not a failure lazarus
life is not a race that you win or lose
only compare yourself to yourself
then i am hopelessly worse at everything
compared to what i once was
you have hardly aged yet i am old and grey
tiberius is dead but his spirit haunts me
every night in my dreams he grabs me by my ankles
like the robber sciron he tosses me off the cliff
like theseus you can use your strength to toss him over
let us wrestle arm to arm to prove how strong you are
there on the cave floor we arm wrestled
lazarus pushed my arm down
see you are stronger than me i said
something that you can remember me for
letting me win is your final triumph
but you see jesus in my eyes
the secret future that you could never see before
the one thought that i have left is a choice
the one life that i can control now

must be fulfilled in my death
you will not stop me now
he said as he dove over the edge
*

Lazarus did not join the holy spirit
Those who take their own lives
Do not go on to join the group voices
Yet wherever Jesus is his friend Lazarus will be
Jesus is loyal through death through time
The love of Jesus is more than the Holy Spirit
*

even without the holy spirit
at the right time
the wind blew time to return to jerusalem
lene did not believe in wind blowing
she said she had heard all my stories too often
her mind no longer supported my missions
she did not like my music anymore
why not just enjoy our gardens
it is not yet time for heaven on earth I said
stay and make perfume to delight my return
you are always gone on some voyage
leaving me lonely is your way of life
always having eye embraces with other women
you never loved me only me never two as one
you loved niki and I am just a substitute
my love is outgoing and constantly expanding
my love for you is in my innermost circle
you are the white star in my eyes
that circles the black centre
why is it always about your eyes jesus
everything is always about you
you could be just an ordinary man
but that is not enough is it
lazarus was right
you have to be better than everyone else
let me tell you jesus if you go on this trip
i may not be here when you get back
parting is never easy
yet you are always in my heart

my duty to my followers calls me to the holy land
*

great michael carried me
accompanied by astron
my strong willed daughter carried by gabriel
north and east
at the edge of a frozen sea
a white bear and her cub leaped over ice flows
reminding me of the time before
a frozen land the north star cave
stopping there i could now hear voices of prayer
my mind reached great distances to listen and speak
after resting for a day we again flew
the sun never setting long days
a cold voyage over an ocean
to a hard land with white skinned people
blonds and red headed red bearded warriors
landing by the sea near a larger city
we found the people very friendly to us
once they overcame their first fear in seeing us
overcoming their instinct to fight
yet they loved my words and my message of peace
for a year we stayed and taught them
leave your odin and thor and false gods
come and sing in the temple of jah we built
a temple of song made of wood like the congo one
here astron met a man and they fell in love
he was a king and she accepted to be his queen
to stay and teach the people the way in
gabriel said she would stay for a time too
protecting astron from the many war worshippers
protecting my daughter from the angel satan
protecting my blood line
*

michael and i flew on
flying across gaul and along the coast
to highlands near rome where michael hid
from prying eyes to give me time
to allow me to search out people
hear news first hand

out of mouths instead of minds
my name was known by many
secret written gospels were circulating
some of my words and parables recounted
my teachings and stories about me written
especially the story of my crucifixion
these gospel words also distressed me
missing some stories
inserting obstacles to the way in
false stories stumbling blocks
an organization was growing
my true gospel was needed
but jah urged me to wait
answer only personal prayers directly
not intervene in directing how the faith grows
LET IT HAPPEN JAH SAYS HAVE PATIENCE
JAH ALLOWS THIS TO COME TO PASS FIRST
FOLLOWERS ARE PERSECUTED AND TORTURED
THE WAY IN IS AN UNDERGROUND STREAM
ONLY JAH KNOWS WHEN IT WILL EMERGE
LET EVERY CREATURE CREATE STORIES
THE WAY IN IS A MIRROR THAT INSPIRES LOVE
IT IS NOT THE ACTUAL LOVE
THOSE WHO SHOW LOVE HAVE NO ENEMIES
yet satan has been powerful in rome
his mind affecting many high rulers
while underground my followers
were slowly growing in number
the emperor the princeps nero
delighted satan by setting fire to rome
blaming my followers for the burning
words of the burning words in their hearts
were used against them
nero had tortured and crucified many
michael and I flew right at nero
in his palace we woke him
through the doors in his mind we flew
condemning him to hell
*

Judgment and casting out of souls from hope

Are granted to the Holy Spirit
For grievances against the souls of the beloved
Death remains beyond judgment but guilt and insanity
May be measured out fully to those who act as slaves to Satan
Having no conscience of consequences
*

michael flew me to jerusalem
my brother james led my followers in jerusalem
he welcomed me home
took me to our mother mary
very old and living alone
in the care of my disciple john
the roman legions were marching
no time for visiting exchanging stories and love
throughout the growing flock of followers
everyone must leave jerusalem this very day
everyone must leave the land of israel
john was asked to take mary to ephesus
then retire to patmos island
where I would meet him again
*

The temple was about to be destroyed
The jewish people were to be vanquished
The prayers of those slain or in slavery already
Jehovah answered with comfort not war
The Holy Spirit and Jesus urged the followers to leave Judea
Leave Jerusalem and scatter to other lands
Comfort each other
The holy spirit is not in a temple
Everywhere in the world the living spirit
May be connected through prayer
*

each of my family were known by me
all my followers kept secret
leaving desolate jerusalem
leaving all of judea
heart of the land of jehovah
the lands of israel promised
to the descendants of abraham

*

Seeds of thoughts and visions
Signs of the end of days
In the future the jewish people will return
From the scattered places they hide
Like chicks returning to mother hen
That will be a sign that Jesus is present
That Jah now Jehovah always keeps his promises
The return of the jews
Will be a sign of the end times

*

this was my message to my jewish followers
the true end of the world
the end of time is a different end
no person knows what hour it will be
yet those who see the belly rise will know
to expect the beginnings of labor
only when the good news of the way in
has been preached to every group of people
then the doors close and the way in is sealed
the day of final time will come
suddenly as if a child is born
those who follow until the end of their days
those who endure for my sake will be saved
if not for the word
the whole world would end
at the end of days all the people alive
the number alive will be beyond comprehension
billions of people will be alive
their growth overwhelming the earth
killing other kinds of creatures
humans will have the power of gods
they would destroy the world
if not for my love
some humans will have powers like jah
powers of creation and destruction
it will happen at the same time as new energy
energy only seen in the sun before that time
comes to earth at the hands of humans
a third sign of that time will be a return

of humans all speaking the same language
just as in the days of the tower of babel
humans will again build towers of babel
all speaking the same languages
understanding each other
instant understanding by everyone
humans destroying the earth claiming to be gods
they will not believe in any god but themselves
they will war with god and the earth itself
those who are saved because of the word
those who follow me
their spirits dwell with me beyond time
inside the house of jah beyond place
jah will bring us in love to all the earth
bless us with a new eden to live in
a new heaven right on earth
a new temple of the spirit of love
a new start of time under my guidance
everyone will be free of fear
wickedness and pain will dissolve
the earth will have a wealth of creatures
all sharing an eden in harmony and love

*

Can Jesus save the believers in Jah the creator
Save the earth from total destruction
Remember this
The Holy Spirit sent out the thoughts
As a prophet Jesus predicted
The destruction of the temple

*

john shared news of my old disciples
funny stories of good times
most of my followers had met mortal end
my flock scattered but still growing
a wild flock that i left alone to grow
john and i shared mind speech easily
michael spent several days with john
he gave john some of the vision medicine
john was to write a revelation

of his visions with michael
which the holy spirit was allowing
when we left i hugged john again
my last hug before the end of his days
his thought prayers would be answered by me directly
his revelation of the future to be spread
as a written warning sign
a prophesy in symbolic words
until the time jehovah allows
*

michael carried me along
first stopping on our mountain
a prayer contact with jah on mount sinai
then repeating the golden ring voyage
visiting every ring bearer still alive
or seeking out the person given the ring
searching minds searching hearts
telling my stories my gospel of jah
on the banks of the ganges
meditating on the dead
on banks of lake naboom
then along the mekong and yangtze rivers
visiting the civilization of the han
time again with a snow tiger
a daughter of my departed sheama
for years we travelled east
finally back to the thunderbird lands
another scroll would be needed
to contain those stories of lands revisited
old and new friends found
it is enough that this scroll is written
to be reborn from a hidden tomb
near the new eden garden
grown by lene and our family
fruits and vegetables nuts and berries
cherries cucumbers carrots and melons
peaches almonds grapes figs and dates
the eyes of new followers
finding me near their own gardens
*

at the age of one hundred and twenty five
the angel jah came for me
took me with him
to a meeting with satan
**WE ARE GOING TO WRESTLE
ANGEL BEING AGAINST ANGEL BEING
WITH YOU JESUS AS THE PRIZE**
jah explained the contest
was to be held every
three hundred and sixty five years
one year for every day in a year of time
**GUIDANCE OF THE ESSENCE OF THE BEING
THE SPIRIT OF YOU JESUS IS HELD BY THE WINNER
BETWEEN EACH PERIOD OF TIME**
do i have a say in this
**NO IT IS IN THE REALM OF ANGEL SPIRITS
JEHOVAH HAS ORDAINED IT**
what does the holy spirit say
THIS IS NOT A DEBATE JESUS
if you lose the power of satan takes me
HAVE NO FEAR

*

we flew to a barren island
where jah set me down on a plateau
satan was waiting off to the side
his plumage was iridescent dark rainbows flashing
like oil on dark water reflecting sunlight
as he spread his wings to attack jah in the air
jahs feathers were brighter clean colors
rainbows from within rather than reflections
both birds rose above me and circled
then dived at each other colliding
grabbing each other holding tightly
rolling and twisting as they fell to the ground
both stood apart eye to eye
then smashed into each other
bounced apart and I found myself between them
brushed aside by jah i reeled away
satan used the distraction to slap a wing
against the head of jah

knock him over and pounce up on his chest
jah was pinned and satan counted
one two three
*

AS THE WINNER OF THE FIRST BATTLE
THE PRIZE BELONGS TO ME
TO DO WITH AS I WISH
JESUS IS TO BE PLACED OUT OF TIME
OUT OF COMMUNICATION
OUT OF BEING HIMSELF
OR BEING ANY OTHER SPIRIT FORM
NOW REMEMBER YOUR GREAT GRANDFATHER
ON THE SIDE OF YOUR FATHER
WAS MY FATHER SATAN TOO
THERE WILL BE A NEW CONTEST
EVERY THREE HUNDRED AND SIXTY FIVE YEARS
A CHANCE FOR YOUR FEMALE SIDE TO WIN
IF THE TIME COMES WHEN JAH
CAN OUT WRESTLE ME
*

in my consciousness five days passed
each day a new match to witness
after five losses jah finally won
outside of my consciousness the five days
were eighteen hundred and twenty six years
in contemplation time
a time of silence and shadow shade
has covered the way in for a time
darkness deep darkness in a cave
like a bear hibernating asleep
my words to be resurrected
by the thought of jah at the time to be
the time my words will come to life again
words about the full life that is mine
words dug up in a tomb of time
words on a buried gold scroll
words of my heart beating
je hov ah je hov ah
we will have heart beat harmony

my wandering words finally written
words shared in minds
words shared in heartbeats
together with jah every beat
**JAH SAYS MY POWER IS ETERNAL LIGHT
SHINING IN THE HOLY SPIRIT**

*

A body dissolved in the north star cave
Where prayers are heard and answered
Jesus the spirit again answers in the new being
Spirit thoughts are again continuing to travel
To care for the flock of followers
Even without a body the words
The spirit will be in every heartbeat
Just as angels hear invisible prayers and reply
So shall Jesus hear the thoughts and prayers
Of those who believe and pray to us
The followers know this truth through the Holy Spirit
In the end of time Jesus is freed from Satan
Satan will be a loser from his own hell cave
His being and his power are doomed
His way out his black hole sealed shut

*

the earth will breath life
harmony vibration to extend time
shared life with all beings
all life in water on land and above
breath in the air to gather forever
all people and animals
birds trees insects organisms
pulse together in harmony
caring for each other
as each does for itself
as the way in
to the heartbeat of the living earth
angels have gone from the living earth
only spirits remain
as part of the holy spirit
many other kinds are no longer alive
at the same time as jehovah allows

a nation of jewish people to be reborn
the world knows that the time is now
a descendant of the line of jesus
has been born in that time
the smell of hope from me
the love that is my message
words true to my heart
creating this gospel healing
as saga songs of jesus
songs about me i am sending to you
through a man called way in
who will have my eyes
to eye embrace my being
smell my tears
taste my words
hear my music
wear my ring
touch my love
always love

Jesus